Casual Observations

Attempts to Rethink What
Appears to Be Obvious

Kakanar

ISBN: 0692028854
ISBN 13: 9780692028858
Library of Congress Control Number: 2014906999
KAKANAR, Glendale, CA

Contents

On National Public Radio, there is a program called "This I Believe." Much similar to that is this effort of mine to put to page things that I have grown to believe in. Some of these ideas or thoughts have been mulling inside my head for almost three decades. Some have attained their form more recently. The topics I have taken on are varied, but I'm writing this because there is an absence of this particular form of opinion or thought on these subject matters in common public domains. My goal is ultimately two-pronged: first, to put to paper my beliefs so that in the future, should I lose the capacity to articulate my thoughts, then at least this text will speak for me, and second, to start a conversation, not a debate, and not an argument. In the end, a person's personal beliefs are his or her sole businesses, not up for validation or criticism by anyone else. However, through conversation, ideas and opinion can be improved upon by each person in his or her own time. Thought, if stagnant or unchanged, can become irrelevant. But if it retains its form in the face of constant challenge, then it will become more pertinent.

Everyone views life a little bit uniquely. We all have our own story to tell and observations to make. The way I conceptualize it is that life is a multifaceted crystal and each of us has the capacity to look in through a limited number of facets of the crystal. The more we hear from others of what they see, the more wholesome our understanding of the workings within the crystal becomes. This is my view into the Crystal of Life. It is an observation interpreted within my own personal thought paradigms.

I do not want this to be an exercise in academic discussion. I want it to be a compilation of thought and what can be arrived at just by applying thought to some casual observations of life. Specifics have been avoided deliberately as they tend to obfuscate the intent. Facts are points on paper. Insufficient facts tend to confuse, and too many tend to distract. I am interested in the patterns that emerge from observations. These are not absolutes but rather subjective to the observer's point of view. They may or may not have any relevance to others, but they are relevant to my point of view. Maybe there might be others who perhaps have had a similar observation.

This is work in progress and will remain so.

Finally, this book is dedicated to my primary source of strength, those who have helped in creating my thought paradigms, my parents. Also, it is my hope that it will provide a measure of context for my aspirations and dreams embodied in my three daughters. May they succeed where I have failed.

one

Wisdom: Who is The Wise One - The Giver or The Taker?

I do not remember when I actually first formulated that specific question. But it has always bothered me that the credit of being wise has always fallen on the shoulders of the most passive of individuals. I guess while growing up listening to the mythological tales from India, at some point in time I began to question the so-called wisdom of the sages in the stories, as despite being wise, they neither could nor would prevent all the happenings of loss, tragedy, and suffering through war and deception. If they were so wise, how come all they ended up doing was to be witnesses to human folly repeated endlessly through time? In India we are taught to be deferential to our gods and gurus to a fault. When the Indian mathematician Ramunajam made his mathematical prowess known to the world, he credited the influence of his family goddess, who had come to him in dreams and taught him what to write. Compare that to the experience of Kekule who had a dream of a snake eating its own tail and derived from it the structure of the carbon in benzene molecule. Both were individuals of exceptional abilities, and yet one conferred the acts of wisdom to a higher power. We, on the other hand, do not have any illusions about whether they both were steeped in wisdom within their respective fields.

Let's imagine a typical wisdom exchange. A holy man in deep mediation sits under a tree on the outskirts of a village. Every so often he arouses from the meditative trance to interact with the world, especially with the curious few who have ventured to seek his views on their worldly affairs. Invariably there are a few who have brought their daily burdens to lay at his feet in the hope that perhaps he might offer them some insightful advice that will help them to resolve the issues.

Usually his discourse begins with an earnest hearing, followed by some probing questions, and then some deep, silent contemplation/prayer session followed by his declaration of the prescription for the unfortunate's life problems. This pattern is repeated time and again. Of all the people he speaks to and advises, some will go home and attempt to follow through with his advice. Of these some will actually see a reversal of their fortunes, some more dramatically than others. There are others who might not see many long-lasting benefits. The reputation of the sage will be dependent on many factors, but the most critical of these will be the success rate of his advice in having helped someone and how well it gets publicized by his followers.

This scenario can be played with different actors in different settings—a priest or rabbi in a religious congregation, a therapist and his or her clients in an office, a school counselor in the school environment.

All of these cases involve essentially two parties—one with some vexing problem that needs an answer, and the other, who is apparently the one with the wisdom/training/skills/intuition to be able to offer a suggestion of a remedial action.

It has traditionally been the case to call the one giving the advice the wise one. But really, who is the real person with wisdom in the exchange?

To illustrate this point, let us assume that there are two individuals with identical problems. The problem can be anything: financial, personal, social, whatever. Both individuals approach the same "wise" man for advice. Given that their problems are practically identical, the solutions are also identical. Now, to add a wrinkle to the story, one of them is suffering from a mental handicap, making it a little difficult for that person to comprehend the "wise" man's advice with the same clarity. Will the end result of this type of exchange be identical or different? It will obviously be different, and yet the only difference between the two exchanges was the mental capacity of one of the recipients of the advice. Now let's replace the individuals' mental competency differences with linguistic differences. In the exchanges between the "wise one" and the persons with the problem, one of the individuals will understand the discourse better than the other. Again, the end result will obviously be different. Finally, if the "wise one" offers advice that is identical to two individuals with similar backgrounds and with similar problems, with no differences with either person's mental or language competencies, in the execution, is it conceivable that one may be more successful than the other? Probably. Aptitude and ability to apply the advice is a human variable.

Now to modify the above thought experiment with another twist; this time the variation is on the "wise" man's end. In each of the above scenarios, the wise one modifies the advice he gives. He tailors the advice to each person based on his or her individual uniqueness, and then *voilà*, his advice begins to produce the results intended.

Did the wisdom manifest when the sage spoke or when the people in dire need of advice heard the advice? Alternatively, if the words of wisdom were uttered in a large auditorium full of people, would the advice have sought out its recipients for the desired effect, or would the advice be rendered useless as it was not delivered with any specificity? On the contrary, if the same individuals seeking help had heard similar words in an out-of-context situation, would they have been able to use it to their advantage? I argue that the second set of circumstances is more likely, wherein it might lead to the receiver of the information becoming enlightened and acting upon the advice, affecting a positive change. Serendipitous epiphany! Both scenarios are based on luck, allowing for the right connections to be made. But in the cases of individuals looking for advice, they are more likely to be receptive to the appropriate words than to the effect of those words by themselves on random strangers.

Then, where does the true merit of wisdom rest? Is it in the corner of the sage giving the advice, or is it in the corner of the person who is seeking resolution? Metaphorically, if advice were to be imagined as a seed with the potential for great change and growth, then the mind of the seeker of wisdom can be imagined to be the soil in which that wisdom must germinate and take form. Here the success of the thought implantation is more dependent on the nature and fertility of the individual's mental soil. In the world we live in, "thought seeds" are a dime a dozen. Every time we open our mouths to speak intelligently or otherwise we are all generating a thought seed. Sometimes these seeds find fertile, appropriately prepared, eagerly awaiting mental soils where they can germinate to their full potential. But more times than not they get wasted in the wind. Alternatively, let me offer a modification to the above example in that the *thought-solution* idea in seed form and the fertile soil all exist in the mind of the one with the problem yet to be solved. Advice can then best be considered as that which will stimulate the seed to develop, like water or fertilizer. Everyone who engages in speech is disseminating the fertilizer for growth, but when the thought seed is absent in the right soil, all the fertilization in the world will be inconsequential.

In the example where a therapist takes the role of the learned sage, his or her efficacy in transacting a successful therapy session is, to a large extent, predicated on his or her ability to read the problem accurately with empathy and patience, and then to prescribe a course of action that he or she deems is individually tailored to the needs of the person with the problem. Most in this field will agree that this is, in essence, the secret of their success. So, in the example, is the more effective therapist wiser or simply better trained and experienced? This is also applicable to the holy man under the tree in the outskirts of the village. He has attained his "wizened" world view through previous experiences and the study of the human condition within religious/cultural mythological contexts. Is he then truly wise or just experienced?

By contrast, look at the innate wisdom that is essential on the part of the solution seekers to appreciate the value inherent in the advice being provided. It is their ability to grasp the content of the advice and act on it that makes the advice that much more pertinent.

How many times in our lives have we encountered situations where when we offered advice, and it was most often ignored, making us roll our eyes in frustration? How many "I told you so" moments have we been through? In all these scenarios, there is the person with the problem and there is the knowledgeable "sage" offering insightful apt and appropriate advice, and yet the end result is lacking in any remedial action. In these instances, was it because the sage was not wise enough or because the one with the problem was not suitably equipped with wisdom to recognize the value of the advice being given?

Words of wisdom acquire their status only if they are acted upon to produce the desired result; when action is absent, the words have no real value. Since action is in the controlling hands of the person with the problem, isn't their innate wisdom a prerequisite to whatever wisdom is inherent to the advice?

So who is truly the wise one, the one giving the advice or the one receiving the advice?

two

Cancer Prevention: Is It Really Possible to Prevent Cancers?

Cancer is a word that has many interpretations. For some the word is almost always the equivalent of a death sentence proclamation, and for some it has no concrete meaning. We have known of people who have lived recklessly, gotten cancer, and recovered, and at the same time we have heard of children who have been cut down before their prime despite heroic treatment measures. Ever since I learned about the human body, genetics, and variations possible through mutations, I have always wondered if a cancer cure is a misnomer. What about cancer prevention?

This is not a researched informative write-up as much as a loose interpretation of the general laws of genetics and at the end a pondering of a hypothetical.

What is cancer? Is it really possible to prevent cancer? Treating cancer and managing patients with cancer are possible, but can one actually **prevent** cancer? A lot of things apparently cause cancer. Most times the medical research community seems to be engaged in the endless search for the exact mechanism of cancer formation so that they may somehow interfere with it and thereby stop the cancer-forming process. At other times they are furtively compiling lists of items that help in the creation, growth, or spread of cancer so that they may attempt to prevent exposure to these agents. But is eliminating all theoretically possible cancer-causing agents from the environment enough to prevent cancer formation?

What is cancer? Simply put, these are cells that no longer adhere to the rules that apply to other cells. Cancer-causing agents, also known as carcinogens, either cause, aid, or abet the mutations that change the cells sufficiently to make them cancerous. Anything from sunlight to man-made chemicals can theoretically trigger cancer and cause changes. The old listing of cancer-causing agents was known as the **"7 S"**: *Sunlight, Sepsis, Spices, Spirits, STD, Sharp edges (chronic irritation), Smoking*. If, in a hypothetical scenario, all possible cancer-causing agents are eliminated, will the organism be able to survive to a ripe old age without the danger of ever contracting cancer?

A good photocopier can reproduce a copy with very high fidelity. If a copy of the copy was to be made on the same copier, depending on the quality of the copier, another high-fidelity copy, identical to the original, might be produced. If this were to be repeated a third time and a fourth time, the resulting copies would begin to show sight differences when compared to the original. This loss of fidelity is to be expected even from the best copiers. Now imagine the rate of copying of cellular genetic material that takes place day in and day out with hardly any loss of information. Over the years, with thousands of instances of copying occurring, it is again within reason to expect some mistakes in the copying to happen. This is the genesis of mutant cell strains. Some of these changes produce unexpected positive changes, which are then reinforced in successive copying. These serendipitous changes account for the evolutionary improvements in an organism. Some, on the other hand, result in defective cell development.

Every mutant cell that is produced faces tremendous odds to survive. The first hurdle to cross is one of simple viability. Most alterations to the genetic database render the cell less resilient, more vulnerable, and eventually incapable of surviving or continuing with the act of cell multiplication. Those that get past this hurdle then have to compete with other normal cells for nutrients. If the mutation has made the cell deficient in any way, then, competitively speaking, it is pushed out. Then there is the hurdle of not being attacked by the host's immune system.

Every time changes happen within the genome (genetic database), these changes might also change the surface characteristics of the cell, making it lose its identifiable markers that help the immune cells to differentiate host cells from foreign cells. Normal cells have their activities closely regulated through biochemical signals from the surroundings through an information feedback loop that promotes or inhibits cell multiplication and other activities. Cancerous cell are cells that, through their mutation, have lost these communicative abilities and are, therefore, not capable of being regulated. Finally, if they do survive, then to get established, they need to be able to commandeer the host systems to supply them preferentially to allow for uncontrolled growth. Given the amount of cell replication that occurs in the body on a daily basis, it is conceivable to expect mutant cells to form with fairly high frequency. It is a testament to the hurdles that have naturally been created to deny these cells a fighting chance to survive that cancers are not that frequent in their establishment.

If cancers are a natural result of cell division mistakes, then how can that explain aggressive cancers in children in whom there hasn't been enough time yet for multiple cycles of cell division? Furthermore, children's exposure to so-called cancer-causing agents is not of great significance yet. However, the rate of cell division is at its highest in children, and even more so during growth spurts, which are triggered or modulated by growth hormones. These are periods of accelerated cell multiplication to produce the concentrated phase of body growth. These same growth hormones can also speed up mutational changes. They act akin to adding fuel to a fire. They might be one of the most potent cancer-causing natural agents to exist. While they are meant for the purpose of stimulating tissue development, they can also very non-discriminately fuel the growth of unwanted cells. In children with the propensity for cancer development, the flaw already exists in the basic DNA structure in their infantile cells. These cancers are characteristically very rapid growing and aggressive. Adults who undergo hormone therapy or take recreational steroids run the risk of initiating or helping grow cancers, some very aggressive by the same mechanism.

In fact, the more aggressive cancers are composed of cells that have regressed to an "infantile" form. Life as we know it begins in a single cell, and through multiple cycles of cell division, that single cell grows to become a glob of cells. At this stage each one of these cells has the potential to become any tissue in the body. They are called *pluripotent cells*, also known as stem cells or undifferentiated cells. Then they begin to differentiate into cells with specific function and roles. This change is brought by how a cell reads, copies, or utilizes the stored information in the DNA structure. A set of checks and balances comes into play to guide the modification of these cells into specific tissue cells. During carcinogenesis, this process begins to unravel and sometimes reverses. The more these well-differentiated cells de-evolve, the more they begin to behave like the stem cells, and with loss of communicative control with their environment, these cells become aggressive in growth and parasitic to the host tissues.

Thus, even if all possible forms of cancer-causing agents are removed, will the simple act of routine cell multiplication, in time, result in errors that will cause a cancerous strain with high viability probability to rise and become established? It has been recently determined that DNA structure shows age-related changes with time, sort of like getting wrinkles. The more distorted the DNA strands become, the greater the accumulation of defects, which are either not recognized or eliminated. In most of the people who die from other causes, the question arises: Did these people have immunity from cancer, or did some other form of death overtake the probability of cancer? Hypothetically if these people had been provided the ability to survive past other natural and unnatural causes of death, sooner or later would they have run into some form of cancer? Maybe. Is cancer, then, an alternate expression of life, a by-product of the simple act of living, an offshoot of the natural living process, yet ironically one that can end it also? In an ideal environment where the effects of disease and sickness have been eradicated or at least rendered ineffective to affect the outcomes of most lives, the ultimate definitive way to prevent cancer appears to be the cessation of life itself. In time the propensity of other things that could go wrong, which could eventually lead to our demise, would become high enough that cancers or preventing them might have less relevance.

A cancer cure is a misnomer in the sense that most cancer treatments aim, at the very least, to contain cancerous growth followed by managing its evolution and, if lucky, putting it into some form of stasis or remission. There is always the possibility of cancer reawakening, and sometimes in a more aggressive form. The best outcome of treatment is that it removes every last vestige or remnant of cancer tissue in the body. Such a complete, excision-style cure is feasible in only a percentage of cancers. But even such "cures" do not prevent a repeat cancer formation in the same tissue-organ or in another. In other words, there are no drug regimens or lifestyle modifications that can prevent a cancer from arising at some point in time.

three

Is Racism Second Nature To Humans?

In late 1970s while riding on a public transport bus in a city in South India, I over-heard a strange observation made by a young man to his friends. He was commenting on how he thought people of African descent were like monkeys. He was perhaps alluding to the color of their skin and not their facial features. The irony of the situation was that the young man voicing the opinion had one of the darkest skin tones I had ever seen, even by Indian standards. Another perplexing observation one makes in a country like India is that despite the great abundance and diversity of religions, the nation has been racked by frequent upheavals of communal violence. It is one of the most religious countries in the world, with a relatively robust secular government, and yet it is and was a land of extreme violence, if not in action then in thought. I have always been perplexed by our ability to discount our darkest tendencies toward other fellow humans on the flimsiest of excuses, yet we are eager to call others deroga-torily, as if by doing so we can feel superior.

One of the critical elements of our human nature that allows us to progress is our ability to differentiate and make choices based on the inherent merits and predictions of consequences. This ability to differentiate helps us to adapt, prepare, and survive. There is also another trait closely aligned with the capacity to differentiate, and that is the capacity to discriminate. This is where one assigns a positive or negative value to an object or process.

The choice to locate a dwelling on high ground, especially in a flood-prone area, is an example of the capacity to differentiate between good and bad options. The choice to eat poultry and not cattle because of the cultural-religious significance of the cow is a discriminating choice.

The area where discrimination causes problems is when it is applied to fellow humans. *To **differentiate** among your fellow humans is not only good but also worthy of being encouraged.* Here we run smack into the conventional notion of equality of humans. The concept loosely quoted and believed by most people is simply put as "All humans are equal to one another." There is nothing more offensive to anyone who understands the value of individual uniqueness than that statement. To put it simply, no individual is equal to another. Each has his or her unique set of skills, failings, memories, and paradigms, which cannot be equated or even compared to another's. In some area one might be superior to others, while in other areas one might be completely out of depth. Therefore, all the concept of equality hopes to offer everyone is equal opportunities to live up to or not live up to the fullest capacity of one's own potential. Where we end up economically or academically, or in any other mode of comparison, is based purely on the consequences of our aspirations, efforts, and luck, of course. In other words, the playing field, theoretically, should be a level playing field with no one suffering as result of discriminatory policies. The concept of differentiation is still vital because that is how we can make our choices of people we want to interact with. Selecting candidates for a job is a differentiating process within the paradigm of the concept of equality. Denying someone's ability to apply for a job based on value judgments such as color, language, race, sex, etc., is a classic example of discrimination.

Racism is a variant form of discrimination. Unfortunately, it is prevalent universally across the globe, in every culture and country. It is not merely a crime of the light-skinned against the dark-skinned. It begins with the encountering of an unknown identity. The initial reaction to this encounter is usually a combination of curiosity and fear. If curiosity is more potent, it might lead to a more pleasant outcome, one that involves new knowledge and understanding and maybe even appreciation and eventually affirmation. If fear is the predominant reaction, then it will lead to a person's need to move away from the new identity and also to assign negative values to the new identity in the hopes of justifying the person's need to react negatively on the basis of fear. Ignorance begets fear, and fear leads to discrimination, wherein the individual is reidentified with a perceived sense of danger, and this in turn justifies any aggressive, hostile action taken against the individual. The irrational response is one of anger and hate. The concept of racism is thus fully established.

To fear the unknown is a survivalist trait that has accompanied our evolution from the long-forgotten cave-dwelling days. When we encounter a potential hostile situation, our instinctive fight-or-flight response kicks in. Flight is usually preferred to fight as it has a higher probability of an outcome that may not be deadly to self. Fight is the option when flight is not realistic. In human social encounters, circumstances sometimes make the flight response impractical, or a nonoption. The only other option left is to be eternally in a state of preparing for a fight. There is, of course, the third option of trying to understand the person who is "alien" and in the process dispel the need for a fight-or-flight response. But that is a rational approach, while the fear response is an emotional one. Emotions outrank rational thought in most instances.

Would this imply that all humans are inherently capable of racism overtly or covertly? Unfortunately, this seems to be true. The only set of circumstances that prevents a racist mindset is one in which a person has attained familiarity in dealing with people and cultures that are vastly different from his or her own and, through multiple encounters, has allowed those encounters to reset his or her personal paradigms or where he or she has controlled fear responses and has rationalized out of his or her thinking the need for fear when encountering someone foreign.

The ability to maintain a progressive, open-minded, and curious outlook can consume a lot of personal energy. Each time one encounters a new entity, one has to be vigilant about an innate tendency to be cautious and suspicious and even the need to be, initially, skeptical and hostile. Our natural state is the one in which we are as economical as possible with our efforts and energy commitments. In our youth we are freer with our personal time and commitments. This might explain why it is a lot easier to be open-minded and flexible when one is young. When we are young, we can expend endless amounts of energy to maintain relationships with others. We are more accommodating. It is also the age at which a life of endless possibilities lies ahead and making connections and exploring the environment are all essential to future prospects. To do all that, one has to have an inexhaustible reservoir of personal energy, a flexible mental attitude, and an explorer's spirit. As one get older, it is noticeable that most individuals tend to become more set in their ways and less flexible. The primary reason for this has to do with the decreased amount of energy available to form and maintain commitments. As we age, our bodies and minds get tired more quickly. With loss of youth, there is also a loss of the desire to waste time and energy. It makes practical sense to clearly mark the confines one is comfortable to exist within and then stick to them. This is why people tend to become more conservative in their outlook on life as they age and become reluctant to be induced to change their positions. Racist or discriminatory thought also becomes easier to accept. It is another way of surrounding oneself with like-minded people, where not much energy has to be dispensed to understand someone.

At the individual level, one may be excused for having racist tendencies, especially if he or she harbors these as private thoughts with no bearing on the life of the larger public. It is when the same tendencies become institutionalized and promoted as policy, with the implication on many lives, that they become recognized for their potential to promote not just discrimination but also hatred.

During the conditions that led to Second World War, the institutionalization of racist policies was possible because the private misgivings of individuals was amped up by the willing and contributing efforts of the Nazi machinery. If the government had not participated or promoted the race-based theories, the Holocaust would not have materialized. Likewise, the government could not have legitimately executed such an efficient administration of racist policies and programs if it did not have the covert and overt collusion and support of some of the inherent racist ideologies from within the population. The Rwandan genocide was conducted by one group of individuals against another group from the African bloodline. Here the discrimination had nothing to do with the color of the skin or the race of the people but rather with tribal bloodlines. During the partition of The Indian Subcontinent, the genocide that was precipitated along the newly formed border was also a form of discrimination. Ironically, in all of these examples the fear of an alien identity was really not that alien. The fear was against a group of individuals with whom there had been close interactions, sometimes going back a few generations. The genocidal tendencies did not manifest themselves suddenly in the population. These tendencies manifested themselves because of a theology of discrimination against the "others" that had existed and was ignored or condoned by the population at large. There had to have been whispers of how unideal things were because of the presence of certain interlocutors in the society and how much better it would be if they all went away.

How then does this form of hatred fueled behavior square with the earlier representation of what constitutes racism? In these examples, the acts of violence are within a particular race or ethnic group. Discriminatory behavior is easily adopted when individuals are dissimilar in physical appearance. This is how race-based discrimination—"typical racism"—arises. But the same mechanisms are at play when discrimination is based on other attributes also. It is our uniqueness and our curse as humans that we can acquire identities of different shades. Any individual can have multiple identities. The one based on the color of the skin or racial origins is only one of them. Identities can be based on the country of origin, the religion of preference, sexual orientation, wealth class, vocations and hobbies, indulgences, etc. It is, therefore, very well within the confines of what is probable, if not possible, that people with similar makeup and outlook can be rendered foreign just by acquiring a new attribute. In other words, if we want to find something to quibble over, to start a point of conflict, we don't have to look too far. If I were to switch my religious inclination, I would suddenly become qualified for being treated with suspicion, and in worse cases with prejudice, and I would be discriminated against. If we keep reducing our circle of acquaintances based on our differences with them, it will eventually result in a circle of one and nobody else.

Legislating against discrimination or racism goes only as far as the population is willing to adhere and support the reform being instituted. If the people are largely of the mind-set to ignore the rationale and the specifics of anti-discriminatory laws, then these laws will merely exist on paper with no real consequences. Look at the caste culture in India. Despite laws being written to abolish caste-based policies, in many parts of the country caste-based dealings still continue. Besides, forcing people to behave in a politically or legalistically correct manner does not help eradicate the innate tendencies for discrimination and racism. It merely drives these tendencies underground, and they continue to exist, either subliminally or quietly, among like-minded people.

The arrival of the Internet and the active interaction among people through the blogosphere has in some instances helped to revive latent racism. The Internet has accorded anonymity to the people, and this has in turn made them comfortable to dabble in their darkest and deepest mind-sets. Thinking before committing thoughts to record is no longer the norm. Lack of consequences and the pleasure one gets by race-baiting and throwing demeaning insults has now been raised to a new level of personal entertainment. The resurgence of discriminatory thought has further been justified by the distorted logic some personalities in the media and political circuit have adopted as a way of furthering their personal agendas by stoking the flames of xenophobia among their fan bases, and this in turn has led to more open expressions of racism. It is now considered acceptable and a measure of honesty to articulate one's thoughts openly, however distorted the rationale maybe, and not be hidden behind a veneer of political correctness.

How does one eradicate the innate tendencies of discrimination? The answer is simple: one does not. Accept that it is in our being to discriminate and be racially prejudiced, and then be ready to commit to a continuous and ongoing education of not just the damages of discrimination in society but also the benefits of fighting it, especially economically. The other element is to institute measures to neutralize the concept of "alienness." Promote programs that increase interaction between not just the diverse groups within the country but also with other nations. Imagine if a fraction of the military budgets of most nations was to be applied to setting up funded foreign study programs. This would force the citizens of the world to interact with one another, and if this could be expanded and cultivated, it would, to a large extent, help in defeating the fear factor that comes from ignorance of another culture and race of people.

four

Guns and War!

Outside of the United States, there is probably not much public discourse on the ownership of guns. Most communities and countries do not have national debates on the pros and cons of gun ownership. The issue is not that the United States has a monopoly on personal firearms ownership or that the United States is the only country uniquely beset with the problems of criminality, or with mentally unstable individuals who are prone to expressions of violence. There are other countries where gun ownership goes back quite a few decades, and the issue of criminality and psychiatric violent people is present in all societies. But what is jarring is the paradox of the United States being the most powerful country, enjoying economic bounty, possessing advanced technologies, and having relatively peaceful living, yet the country is faced with the highest gun-related violence every year.

My personal position on guns was neutral before I came to the United States. Gun questions were never a part of any decisions we had to make growing up. Ownership of guns was not something we debated. In other words, there was no real utilitarian value to guns in average civilian life. As kids we did romanticize about guns in the same vein as playacting or improvisational fantasy making. But it never occurred to us to have an opinion, religious, political, or even intellectual, on this issue. But in the United States any opinion you have is immediately evaluated to fit certain preset positions.

Does any nation really need guns among its citizenry in today's world? Throughout human history we have founds ways and means of destroying each other with ever greater frequency and great success and in ways that no other species seems to naturally do. So the immediate takeaway is that we are the most violent, self-destructive species that has ever evolved. The irony is that we also happen to be the most imaginative and creative of all the species. However, the combination of our creative, imaginative, and destructive skills makes us the most dangerous species. So what logic is there in allowing for the arming of individuals of our species with instruments of death and destruction?

Given that we have this penchant for killing, it makes perfect sense to limit the capacity to kill, especially from a distance, with impunity. A person on a killing spree armed with a knife will only get so far before being killed or tackled into submission. The same person with a gun can stand at a distance and commit the same act with more freedom and confidence. Guns tend to amplify the capacity to kill from a distance unlike any other tool. The training required to become a proficient killer with a gun is minimal. In the days prior to the evolution of the guns, killing had to done with a knife, sword, bow and arrow, or poisons, all of which required some skill or knowledge or required a lot of guile and deception. Guns have expedited the impulsive killing capability. If I were to lose my temper, then in a moment of temporary rage I might be inclined to cause quite a bit of destruction if I had access to a gun. If I am slight of build and do not possess a gun, all the rage in the world would not prompt me to threaten anyone's life as the chances of things not working out favorably for me would be pretty high; I would probably then go for a walk to blow of the steam.

The gun ownership among citizens is of two characteristic types. Among families that have always owned and used guns as part of their everyday living, guns have as much novelty value as a pack of cigarettes or a backpack or farm implements. These are households where there is a purpose assigned to the gun. This ownership is devoid of romanticizing tendencies. With these ownerships comes a compulsory acceptance of the rules of ownership. These rules involve respecting the weapon for what it is, storing it safely, maintaining it, and knowing how and when to load, unload, carry, and use it safely. With the change of times, a lot of the historical role for guns in everyday life has diminished and more often than not has relegated guns to remain idle in the gun cabinet. A gun might be brought out for a planned hunt or as a part of a ceremonial event. The use of the gun in self-defense or in protection of the household may no longer be the primary reason for the gun's ownership.

The second type of gun ownership is the type that justifies ownership of a gun on the basis of personal protection or as an expression of solidarity with some ideal that guarantees ownership as a citizenship right. Some ownership may also be driven by pop culture imagery associated with gun ownership. More often than not, many new owners of guns may not be encumbered by any ownership rules or responsibilities beyond the bare minimum requirements of the law.

This picture gets more complicated with the addition of politics and commerce. When gun ownership rights are essentially determined only by the population who owns or uses the guns, then laws and rules might be written with a mix of pragmatism, involving input from all affected parties. Gun ownership rights has implications for gun owners, law enforcement departments, parks and recreation bodies, non-gun-owning citizens, and regulatory agencies and healthcare facilities that must determine the minimum safety standards that must accompany gun ownership.

But when politics enters the picture, then scare tactics and innuendos are often used to poison the pragmatic discussion that must happen prior to formulating sensible rules of ownership. The gun industry's primary role in the ownership issue is to guarantee an unregulated market where sales can happen with minimal supervision or recordings. This is beneficial for that industry's bottom line. It is their interest that is paramount and not really the interest of the owners.

The want to sell semiautomatics, assault rifles, and sniper rifles, which are actually weapons to be used in a theater of war, shows how skewed the gun ownership debate has become. It has become dictated by the needs of the industry and certain political ideologies rather than the needs of actual gun owners who simply want sensible ownership.

Weapons of war of the past have been relegated to their spots on museum floors or to roles in competitive sports like fencing and archery. Once upon a time, these weapons were customarily carried about on one's person, like today's handguns are carried for decorative or defensive roles. Once wars become infrequent and society as a whole matures, it can be expected that average citizens will require less dependence on personal arms for protection. A mature society should be less dystopian and more capable of providing more personal protection to its citizens. A mature society should have less need to sort out personal difference and quarrels with weapons. Yet in the United States today the logic for increased ownership of guns seems to hedge on convincing everyone that life is more violent and insecure without them. Two hundred-plus years of postindependence existence, having survived one civil war and two world wars, having acquired the biggest economic footprint in the world, having become the richest nation with the best of all technologies available at citizens' disposal, and having a population with one of the highest per capita incomes, has resulted in, frustratingly, a nation that believes itself to be highly crime ridden, violent, and poorly served by its law enforcement agencies, and this view is deplorably pessimistic at the very least. Accounting for those who advocate personal weapons, the nation does not seem to be a civilized nation by any measure of comparison. In the 1980s, when India was having a full-blown civil war on its northwest border, when there were street battles being waged between security forces and ultranationals, the annual death toll to gun-related violence was less than that of the United States, a country not at war with itself but in peacetime, with no terroristic action within its borders and with a population one-third of that of India!

There might be another reason for the "love affair" the United States seems to have with guns. This is a nation that has never really settled down into a full-time peace mode. Peace is a time period when the nation spends more of its capital, energy, and manpower in constructive endeavors from the national level down to the community level. There is minimal to no expenditure in destructive enterprises like wars.

But when wars are thrust upon the nation, either by choice or as a consequence of a foreign policy requirement, then the nation cannot enter into this phase of "quiet introspection." Communities and localities have to deal with the aftermath of constant deployment. These are not the mega cities but rather the smaller towns, which because of their size and disconnected location would otherwise be prone to the negative impacts of economical vagaries.

Every war or military conflict brings with it a price tag in human capital. It sometimes takes one or two generations to rebuild and repair the tears in the social fabric that result from such endeavors. The price the nation pays in capital and in human resources takes time to replenish. To the planners of the war strategy, conducting the conflict to a successful end in victory is the justification for their primary planning and execution. But to the nation, even if it wins a war, there is still a high price to pay, which is the primary reason there are a lot fewer full-blown all-out wars between nations.

But when you subject the nation to a constant state of war, then the effects are seen in the form of a chronic, slow breakdown of the society at large. The need for continuous long deployments away from home puts a heavy strain on the family unit. The death of a soldier destroys his or her family, tears apart relationships. The ones who do return home alive can be expected to suffer from some degree of PTSD, which can in itself put a heavy strain on the family unit. When family units begin disintegrating due to these dysfunctions, then this places strain on society at large.

Alcoholism, drug use, spousal abuse, and divorces all increase. Wars also results in emotional and functional deficits in individuals that make them less predictable socially or in employment circles. This in turn leads to issues of low self-worth, frustration, and eventually distrust. At the same time, the normal checks and balances that would have existed in a close-knit community environment will have gradually been diluted or rendered impotent because communities themselves have been fragmented by the increase of broken family units.

Large, stable family environments are becoming increasingly rare. Societal taboos and behavior red lines have long been violated. The increase of single-parent households, the associated destruction of individual credit histories, and interruptions in education result in a society that is increasingly left with scant tools to repair itself. Imagine the effects on the national level when these conditions that first started to tear the societal fabric continue on for decades. All the anger, frustration, and general lack of support structures will result in conditions in which individuals will choose violence as an expression of their personal angst. (*It is more than a coincidence that the more the nation romanticizes its defense capabilities, the more it feeds the mentality to discuss everything in militaristic terms. Most things in the United States are described in either military metaphors or sports metaphors. Even sports terminology in many instances is a modification of combat terminology.*)

All that is wrong with the current society cannot be simplified as being the result of the nation's love affair with wars, but the Unites States' frequent desire to be involved somewhere globally on a militaristic level has not helped. Ironically, as society becomes more unglued, the more it tends to depend on the defense part of the government for employment and vocational training. Enrolling with the defense department is an inexpensive way of getting job training, especially for those who have not had the benefit of having families with the financial wherewithal to provide adequate education and professional schooling. Despite having a volunteer army, recruitment has never truly been a problem. For some, the appeal to enlist has been their sense of patriotism; for others joining the armed forces is the result of following a family tradition, and yet for others, it is because recruitment opens doors to education, skills training, and possible improved employment prospects. But all of these positive sides of recruitment are best enjoyed during peacetimes only. With the onset or involvement in conflicts, the equation drastically changes. The negatives of being a participant in a conflict build up faster and higher than the positives of recruitment.

How can a nation ever really heal from the wounds of wars? With so much going wrong at the personal level for some of these people, it becomes easy to believe in apocalyptic "End of the World" scenarios and become advocates of preparing for them. Doing so involves not only arming oneself with as much firepower as possible, but also believing in the need to be nondependent on succor from the government. These individuals become prone to absorbing ideologies that are deep in mistrust of any elected authority of governance.

The final point of frustration is the slippery logic in the rationale used to justify gun sales. The Second Amendment to the Constitution is often quoted as the reason for keeping current practices unchanged. No lawmaker will debate the relevance of this amendment in 2013. Yet if the purpose of the Second Amendment was to confer a check on the governing bodies to prevent de-evolution of the republic into a feudalistic or autocratic fiefdom, then it will not work. Unlike the times when the Constitution and its amendments had immediate relevance, the world we live in now operates within a totally different set of rules. The control that the government has over its citizenry in modern times is less through confirming loyalty through submission, but rather through a more subtle, more effective control of the smaller things that affect the lives of the people.

Personal privacy is at its most compromised state. The unscrupulous ways through which the details of individual lives can be probed and monitored by the government and private agencies, if they choose to do so, is almost at an Orwellian level. This loss of privacy is a fault of the conveniences that the public clamored for without a thought for the price they were being asked to pay in order to enjoy them and the ease with which industry lobbyists broke down the legal barriers that would have prevented the mass gathering of personal information that could then be traded for a price. Government control of banking information and taxation penalties and the military-style policing of infringements of the laws, like immigration, labor, and finance, all at the behest of fighting terrorism, have ensured an almost unchallengeable intrusive management of citizens' existence. All of this has been done without even having to fire a shot. All these freedoms were surrendered by the people themselves in a paranoiac psychosis. The main reason that a totalitarian-style government has not yet come into existence is because of a desire on the part of individual members of the same government to live up to some personal ideals that they have always believed in; a second reason is because economically creating this type of government would be the equivalent of killing the Golden Goose.

The logic of capitalism wrapped within the context of patriotism will keep most cynical of thoughts at bay, and this is a better population-managing strategy than imposing autocratic heavy-handed laws on the public. Hypothetically, if the government chose to neutralize any particular segment of the population, it would not have to resort to brute force but rather to subtle control of banking, trade, labor, and government subsidies, etc. Even if the government decided to launch the much-talked-about armed takeover (*among the renegade weekend "militia" movements*), what are the citizens with all the guns at their disposal going to do against threats like drones and stealth fighters and newer technologies in the pipeline? The daily lives of citizens are so intermeshed with technology—technology that can easily be used to punish communities if need be. How is an armed militia going to fight against a government-sanctioned power, water, and electricity freeze? The whole premise of owning guns as a bulwark against nefarious government agencies and activities is a mere Red Herring. The better way is to have a mobilized, informed citizenry tasked with constantly auditing the government. In other words, be involved. Those who challenge the logical validity of the Second Amendment will be called unpatriotic, and those who choose to move the dialogue along on the subject of gun regulations without touching the Second Amendment are simply biding time and pushing uphill on a slick surface.

The second argument for guns is a circular logic argument. The guns are needed to protect the law-abiding citizens from the lawless who have guns. Where do the criminals get their guns? Since they are not manufacturing them, they are buying them from the marketplace, illegally or legally. The marketplace cannot be devoid of guns because then the law-abiding citizens would be at a disadvantage, even though not selling guns would make it easier to prosecute criminals if they were caught with guns in their possession. Besides, the criminal statistics are a confusing mix of career criminals and people who just crossed into criminality based on their first act of using a gun on someone.

The final argument is that guns don't kill people, but people do. Then let's criminalize people from owning guns. If people have such a propensity to kill, then why provide them with tools to commit their crimes with greater confidence and impunity? The foolhardiness of this logic should have become effectively apparent when this type of crime targeted the most vulnerable and precious of the nation's possessions, namely children, and such events have come to pass. It is almost as if life has been trying to send message after message of the ridiculousness of the situation. First it was high school and college-level kids at Columbine and Virginia Tech who suffered murderous rampages. But those events did not produce any meaningful response. Next was the horrendous slaughtering of kindergarten-age children at their school in the Newtown massacre. One would have expected that incident alone to have resulted in the nation rising with one voice and saying, "Enough is enough." But instead, there was the usual parade of apologists to justify the place of guns in the nation's culture. The answer they parroted was to have even more guns in the marketplace!

The irony is that any other product in the marketplace, if it so much as produced an allergic response in people, would result in indignant demands for regulation, and there would be signed petitions to sanction the manufacture of that product and penalize the manufacturers. But guns used to kill with impunity results in the same populace standing firmly to protect the sale of the product with minimal regulation, all on the basis of showing its misconstrued sense of patriotism and selfish clamor for preserving personal freedoms. It is about rights without the inconvenience of obligation. All the while, the manufacturers of guns are laughing their way to the banks.

If the nation wants to provide a healthier and safer place for its citizens, it must first take the risk of imagining something better rather than being a prisoner to its worst paranoia. The fear that life would be less safe if the ownership of personal weapons was banned might be valid. There would be some pain during the transition stages. But every type of freedom has had to be fought for, sometimes with blood. If citizens of nations that succeeded in getting independence from some oppressor had been more concerned about their individual safety and comfort, then there would have been no freedom struggles that culminated successfully. If this nation wants to rid itself of the scourge of senseless gun violence, it too must be prepared to sacrifice its comforts and sense of false security. An entire generation will need to be prepared to pay the price so that future generations can be accorded a safer environment in which to live.

five

Ownership of Thought

Albert Einstein worked on his famous theories while holding a day job at the Swiss Patent Office and eventually published *Relativity: The Special and General Theory*. For the sake of argument, let us assume that he met with a horrible accident that claimed his life prematurely before he could record his genius on paper. Would the theories that he did not get to propose be lost to humankind for good? Would the same theories eventually have surfaced from another mind or set of minds?

In other words, is *thought* unique and singular to every individual, or is it composed of a finite set of permutations that can be created in any mind? We have a planet of over six billion people. Does that mean that we have six billion-plus unique thoughts on any given subject? The answer to that is an obvious no. To clarify, for a lucid and relevant thought to occur on any given subject, there are a few basic criteria that must be met.

The first criterion is a common paradigm within which the thought has relevance—for instance, trying to resolve a theological point of contention within a scientific framework or vice versa may not work. The second criterion is a common information database from which to derive tools to generate the thought. Mathematical challenges are different from challenges faced in the medical field. A third criterion is a clear and comprehensible definition of the point of debate on which the thought is being rendered relevant. Finally, language barriers must not impede the capacity to dwell on the problem.

As long as these criteria exist, the question is, can different minds from different parts of the world eventually conceive all possible permutations of thought on any given problem? Getting back to the Einstein question, the uniqueness of Einstein's thought was not in his thinking up the individual components that make up his theories but rather in the way he connected them together to construct the framework of his theories. In his absence over a period of time, the individual components of his theories might have eventually surfaced in different minds, and then somebody would have had to sit down and stitch them together to make up his or her own version of the theories of relativity.

If thought is not unique to an individual, then how can anyone claim ownership of the thought? If a particular product of an individual's thought has some monetary value, is it right for that individual to monopolize the exploitation of that thought by excluding the potential for monetary gain by any other person who might also arrive at the same thought? This is the concept behind patents and copyright laws. What if the same thought had individually occurred in ten other minds around the world? What makes any one of those individuals recognized as the original owner of that thought with all of its benefits? Is it just that he/ she was the first to announce it or broadcast it and have the thought verifiably recorded as being the first?

Patent rules protect the original owner of a copyrighted product from financial loss due to unlicensed utilization of the owner's product. This brings us back to the fundamental question of ownership of thought. It is not the thought that has reward potential but the actions and products that ensue from that thought. A drug manufacturer probably has, at any given point in time, a variety of formulations stored away in its database reservoir. But only some of these will ever be commercially released. All of those formulas have no value until they are put through the process of testing and optimization and then worked through the economics of manufacturing. Finally, the role of demand for that particular formulation determines the marketability of the product. If by chance a similar formula that independently originated in another lab were to make its entry into the marketplace, should that company's lab be penalized for it? This is where it gets a bit murky with the patent laws. If two identical products are manufactured by two separate entities, then the one that files for copyright first invariably becomes recognized as the owner of that particular product. The originality of thought and the efforts and financial investments made by a pharmaceutical company in the design of the drug is undoubtedly worthy of being rewarded. Therefore, it is perfectly reasonable to penalize anyone who attempts to copy the product on the cheap and turn it over for an easy profit. But what if an identical product was developed independently, with no copying implication, would that also be considered copyright infringement? What if the product is purchased off the market, meaning a fair price has already been paid for it, and then it is modified using another original thought that arises in another individual's head to design a different variation of the drug—can this action also be deemed illegitimate?

This brings up an even more fundamental question: What is the purpose of the thought? Is *thought* not just an expression of our innate desire through our curiosity to try and comprehend our environment? We observe and think when we interact with our environment, and through the thinking process we are, in some small way, trying to comprehend our reality. Everything we do is meant to ultimately lead to a better understanding of who we are, what our purpose is, and where we are heading toward. The simplest questions about our origins, destiny, and destination are being probed in our everyday existence, in every single thing we do. Most times we are not aware of these ongoing queries in our existence because we are so caught up in the mechanisms of daily living that we tend to ignore the subliminal research we are constantly conducting with our environments. The simplest of acts that we do routinely every day may not qualify as research. But just imagine if there was an unplanned observational change in the parameters of things we come in contact with or use. We would be immediately aware of the change, even if we did not understand it. For example, when we go through the daily routine of brushing our teeth, we do the same things every day, such as putting the toothpaste on our brush, turning on the water to wet the brush, brushing our teeth, rinsing our mouth out with water, and spitting the water and toothpaste out. What if on any particular day the water smelled odd or looked discolored? All at once our senses of observation would be tweaked and we would set about finding the reason for the water's smell or discoloration.

While this type of curiosity might be written off as just innate curiosity, I believe in some small measure this is an example of us constantly, but surreptitiously, monitoring the environment we interact with regularly. Familiarity with the environment we interact with has to be reinforced every time we interact with it. Confirming the absence of unacceptable variations to these interactions is comforting. But we do not keep a record of all those interactions. It is when there is variation from the norm that our instincts are alerted and we wonder why the variation happened. How is this informing us about our bigger questions? The bigger questions are usually answered by answering a multitude of smaller questions. We know heat from a flame can burn because we have all felt the heat radiating from the flame. What if we encountered a flame that did not radiate heat? Would that change our understanding of heat and energy? It would fundamentally change a core concept of our reality.

The next question would be, why do we place monetary value on thought? If thinking is as common as breathing air and we do not charge people for breathing air, then why do we insist on being given our due for our thought? The fault apparently has more to do with our society's need to process every interaction in monetary terms. If we lived in a society devoid of the need for money where everything is equal, then the exchange of thought would be free. Everyone with an idea would release the idea, and anyone who so chose to find a use for an idea would put that idea to work. The toil that goes into creating a product from the idea would be rewarded by monetary compensation, but without any limitation on what someone else might do with the product. In other words, downstream modifications to the idea would not have to continue rewarding the "original" thought creator.

six

Rethinking Economy

In the aftermath of the 9/11 attacks in the United States in 2001, the economy began to slow down. The wars that followed in the subsequent years contributed to more financial strain being placed on the nation's economy, and finally in 2006 the nation appeared to give up its ghost and started to come apart at the seams. The fall from grace and the subsequent speed with which the country seemed to have entered into a tailspin of descent caught most by surprise. There were commentaries of economists, TV pundits, and the representatives of the affected industries and banks, all giving their two bits of wisdom and analysis. But most people, despite the extent to which this was covered in the media, still could not get a grasp on what amounted to a functioning economy and what later caused the greatest, wealthiest economy in the world to teeter on the brink of total collapse.

Much like the others, I could not understand the fundamentals by which the economies existed. My naiveté in this area, coupled with having to pay the unwilling price of the mistakes of others, made me look at the teetering economy as an exercise to help make it comprehensible to me. This write-up is the result of that exercise. I don't suppose most people want to be taught Economics 101 in order to understand the basic premises of how economies exist and function. Without a true bearing in these troubled waters, however, individuals cannot be expected to form informed opinions that will allow them to participate in course correction in order to solve one of the biggest economic crises they have had to live through. By simplifying economic functions to some basic elements, we can begin to understand the premise of economy.

What makes up a functioning economy in any society? A functioning economy is the result of all the activity that accompanies and is resultant of the continuous consumption of products and services by all members of the population. In other words, an economy exists because of the consumption activity of society. As long as there are humans, they will need to consume to live. Anything that impedes humans' ability to consume, either due to lack of access to goods or services or lack of means to avail themselves these services and products, will force a freeze on consumption. This in turn will throttle the stimulation of demand and eventually cause the economic engine to seize. Irrespective of the ideology of economic models or management styles, all nations, to be successful, must address the consumption needs of their populations. If any nation fails to do that, then eventually the economy of that nation will crash.

The Pyramid

Every human system eventually attains a pyramid structure to its organization. That is the nature of the human condition. Whether it is skill sets, material possessions, or power, in our societies the population begins to arrange itself into the pyramid shape, where the higher up the pyramid one ascends one will find smaller pools of people with greater accumulation of skills, wealth, and power. Hypothetically, if one could select a pool of individuals, provide them with the same ingredients to subsist, put them on an isolated landmass, cut off all contact with them for ten to fifty years, and then revisit them, one would see how over time this theory of "pyramidization" of society happens. The time it takes for this to happen is not critical. Eventually that society would have a hierarchical structure with those at the bottom, numerically a larger section, supporting numerically smaller numbers of people at the higher levels. The higher up one scales the structure, the greater the accumulation of wealth, power, and material comforts by an increasingly smaller group of people. The people who occupy these higher sections of the structure also begin to exert asymmetrical influence on the decisions in the group that will be more favorable to those in the higher echelons of the organization. Left unchecked, this upward migration of power and control will also result in a simultaneous decrease in value of products and services emanating from the lower layers of the pyramid structure and eventually a reduction in the ability of the people in the lowermost layers to realize a just valuation of their services. This structure will become parasitic to itself with people in the higher stages of the structure exploiting the weaker sections below them. In time this pyramid structure will begin to develop irreversible cracks within itself due to a separation of the *haves* from the *have-nots*.

This sets into motion an elaborate dance of moves and countermoves to gain an upper hand in this tussle. The *haves* will want to protect what has now become, to their way of thinking, their God-given birthright to continue to exploit to the fullest the system to their advantage, while the *have-nots* will want to upset the order completely, shaking it up so that they can reset the societal order and thus neutralize any monopolistic design that has become set in the societal structure. If both sides do not want a violent end to their worlds, then they will have to come to an agreement to allow for some controlled but limited exploitation to continue in return for allowing some individuals of the *have-nots* to climb up the higher levels of the structure through selective promotion. This unfortunately does not fix the inherent flaw in the system and only delays a permanent resolution. In this state, this society is primed for being manipulated by ideologies founded and based on triggering and responding to the basic level of despondency, fear, and mistrust. The simplest division is the first division that took place—that of the *haves* versus the *have-nots*, or the rich versus the rest. The second cleavage in the societal ranks takes place when the solutions proposed to solve this inequity call for either group to give up even more autonomy to an organization, a union or a large governmental body that is supposed to look out for the interests of the less fortunate, or an aspirational model that will tout the very success achieved by the rich as an easily replicable example that even the have-nots can look up to. This is the generic left-versus-right thought model. The first seeks to redress through a large collective body of people who will hopefully do what is in the combined best interest of the people, while the second emphasizes individualism and personal responsibility as the core elements for success along with a hard work ethic.

The Engine and the Fuel

The economy that results from the actions of this distortion of the population structure will be recognized for its individual parts emanating from the different strata of the pyramid. Now, instead of viewing it as one economy, it will be denoted as an economy of the poor versus that of the middle class versus that of the rich and finally the "uber" rich. Any analysis or adjustments proposed will be compromised from the onset because in trying to solve any problem, this economy will also try to preserve the economic pseudo-stratification of the society. In reality, despite looking at society as different sections of people, each section is part of one complex functioning unit and cannot be separately evaluated. If the economy were to be pictured as a running engine, then this notion begins to make more sense. There are various cogs and wheels and gears and drives that make up the engine. Each one of them individually may not amount to much, but even the smallest bolt serves a purpose in keeping that engine intact. There might be components in that engine that are valued significantly higher than other components. But the health and well-being of these expensive portions of the engine are dependent on the efficient functioning of the lesser-valued components. In addition, to make the comparison more realistic, this engine functions in an enclosed environment from which nothing may be removed or added. Everything the engine needs for improvement or for repairs has to be generated from within, and anything that it needs to discard will also need to be done from within. In other words, when we have members of the population who are incapable of contributing to society, we cannot cast them out of society. When they get old, we need to either provide care for them, or else they will negatively influence the functioning of the economy. Likewise, if individuals have committed a crime, they need to be taken out of the contributing class of people and put into an environment where they are still required to contribute to the needs of the society, only then they will be doing so as sentenced labor. Short of death, there is no exit from this enclosed system.

To continue the engine analogy, if the economy was an engine, then the fuel of that engine would be the money flowing through it. The purpose of the money is purely to keep the engine running. If the engine seizes and stops, then the money loses its value. Efficient flow of capital through the engine, therefore, becomes integral to keeping the engine running. Efficient running of the engine in turn will accord value to the money that runs it. Everything must be done to preserve a smooth flow of constant capital through the system. This flow of capital is what accounts for the productivity of the system. If the flow is hindered or diverted, the system becomes cash starved and begins to malfunction.

This style of functioning, when put through the pyramid structure of the society, generates some interesting long-term flaws. Since the power structure is disproportionately more concentrated in the top tiers, the flow of capital eventually begins to pool in the top tiers. Each tier in the pyramid is financially beholden to the tier above it. Since the structure is a pyramid, the capital that is passed on through these transactions ends up in the hands of fewer people. At some point along the hierarchy, the amount of capital being gained far exceeds the existential requirements of the people, and then it begins to pool up. Unless a mechanism is instituted to incentivize the recirculation of this capital, it will progressively be leached out of the system and the system will suffer from the imbalance.

Capital Recirculation

What are the possible mechanisms to ensure the recirculation of stored capital in this system? Basically there are two mechanisms: voluntary recirculation by reinvestments, or starting new enterprises by people who have managed to amass wealth, or involuntary (mandated) recirculation, giving up of a portion of the accumulated wealth through a decree such as taxes. The purpose is to disincentivize excessive accumulation of capital in any section of the pyramid out of circulation from the system, where it has no beneficial purpose to the system.

Voluntary recirculation is an inefficient way of ensuring reentry of capital into the system as it is dependent on the vagaries of individual whims. Some individuals may be more socially conscious than others, and they will look at parting with their hard-earned wealth in the context of the bigger picture of the economy and society, while others might have difficulty justifying the loss of wealth and its associated power unless there is a quid pro quo in the form of greater profit return guaranteed.

Involuntary removal of capital accumulated requires the involvement of an elected or nominated or consensually selected group of individuals to perform the task based on some formula, which again might need to be preapproved by the majority. In addition, this group will also be tasked to inject this capital back into the system in a specific manner to ensure the maximum effect on the economy. **In short, that is the essence of taxation**. The drawback with this method is that since it requires human intervention to set right a problem that has resulted from human activity, it is also subject to corruption and manipulation by the same system. There is potential for the taxes collected to be misused or wasted, and thereby the method would be rendered inefficient in its execution. No matter how many checks and balances are incorporated to prevent waste and fraud, all of those mechanisms are only as effective as the people who run them. **The only realistic solution to this is the active and constant engagement of the entire citizenry to monitor and audit the process. This interaction has to be constant and ongoing, and this means the citizenry has to also be highly educated about the intricacies of the process of governance. Participation of the citizenry sporadically, especially only during selection processes of people or policies, is insufficient to inhibit usurping of the controls by those who want to manipulate the system.**

In today's society the management of accumulation of capital in the hands of the few is through a combination of taxation and offering reinvestment incentives to those who are well off. The debate is not about the need but about the mix of approaches and which should be prioritized. The Right believes in the voluntary capital utilization schemes by the well off and in return wants greater freedom from mandatory wealth removal by government bodies. In short, the Right wants to reward the rich for voluntarily putting their excess capital back into the system and in the process generating more productivity. The Left believes in the taxation-heavy model that allows the government to put the capital to use in a coordinated manner on multiple projects that will affect the largest sections of the population. Their logic is that if the economy can be managed at the basic tiers of the pyramid, then that will keep the higher tiers functioning through the process of upward mobility of capital through the system. In order for this to work, a greater part of the capital has to be cleaved at the top and fed progressively more toward the bottom of the structure—**regulate the top while stimulating the bottom tiers of the pyramid.**

Right versus Left

Both approaches have their own inherent flaws. The approach advocated by the conservative think tanks calls for minimal government interference and regulation and the lowering of taxes on the wealthiest. This is meant to incentivize profit-generating productive behavior, which logically should result in more entrepreneurial activity and its associated increased employment potential. Unfortunately, this only works if both of the following happen: 1) There is a stable or growing economy where the demand for products is good and growing and more importantly is assured to persist into the reasonable future. 2) There is no competitive employment market that can be tapped for the same labor at a much more reduced cost to the business. In the case of the first point, as long as there is demand and predicted growth in the demand, businesses will continue to reinvest in their enterprises (recirculation of capital through the system). Here it is the promise of a financial windfall that guides the reinvestment of capital back into the economy. On the second point, if there is another economic zone that can provide the same labor requirements for much cheaper cost, this will drive the business houses to move their business to that zone and in the process shift the capital out of their native economic zone (flight of capital from the system). This might benefit the bottom line of the individual business, but it does nothing for the money content of the population pyramid.

In other words, the driving force for capital investments in any society has to do with the **return on investment (ROI)**. **The effects of taxation, regulation, or other governmental involvements do not affect the calculations of business decisions as much unless they affect the return on investment significantly.** However, in an economical downtime these would be used as convenient excuses for attempting to change taxation and regulation rules to benefit those who are well off.

The Left-leaning school of thought calls for capital to be collected and redistributed to other sections of society. It may do this by paying for work that needs to be done, such as infrastructure building or repairs, or through paying for civil servants like police, fire departments, hospitals, and schools, and also through establishing social safety nets to prevent lack of assistance to people who are incapable of fending for themselves. All these services require the government to basically be the employer to provide employment. The money for this is largely acquired through the recapture of capital through taxation. The primary criticism of this mode of management is that, since the money is acquired through the taxation method, there is no incentive to be diligent about the utilization of this capital efficiently and honestly. When an enterprise needs to improve its productivity and profit, it needs to work hard to produce the end result. The government, on the other hand, needs to only ensure that tax collection is done accurately and efficiently. In other words, it gets a piece of the pie that the business made with their sweat and blood simply by administering a formulaic taxation. The concept of return on investment does not exist, and hence the accompanying need to be diligent in the way capital is allocated for expenditure is lacking. This leads to waste or rather to inefficient control on the flow of capital through the system. Instead of remedying an imbalance in the system, it might help to create and contribute to it by creating its own zones for pooling of capital. **Any time capital is allowed to pool up in any section of society it is denied the ability to circulate through the system and therefore becomes incapable of catalyzing any productive activity.** The inherent entropy in the human condition means that it will try to find shortcuts in doing any activity and it will also be easily tempted into corruption and inefficiency. The only thing that prevents this from happening is when the actions are wedded to a profit motive within a cause-and-effect model. Of course, active participation by the members of the society to audit and hold those in charge accountable will also deter the unraveling of the government management into chaos and confusion. Over the years, the failure of successive governments to either fix issues comprehensively or even follow through on their verbal commitments has resulted in a loss of faith in government and has generated a lot of cynicism about government officials' effectiveness. Thus, even though the notion of appointing a select group of individuals to manage the redistribution of capital might be well intentioned, the end result is usually one of frustration and leads to sometimes downright loathing.

In reality, though, the Right and Left schools of thought appear to be diametrically in the opposite direction, and there is a lot of comingling that happens, especially if it benefits both mutually. In the government-managed taxation-dependent model, capital redistribution occurs that might also include the entrepreneurs as the recipients. If a particular industry requires some aid in the formative years or if a project is considered high risk but has been deemed a socially worthwhile project, then government assistance in the form of low-cost loans or subsidies to minimize the tax burden might be implemented to help the fledgling or distraught industry survive and thrive. The common problem with this style of government-mandated assistance is that it usually becomes an open-ended arrangement with no clear end date for the assistance. This is another self-created problem for the governmental bodies, because if they administer the rules as per the original understanding, then, if and when the time gets close to ending the assistance program, there will be pushback and acrimonious complaining by the beneficiaries. If the government capitulates to the protests, then it runs the risk of losing all credibility for similar future arrangements. This is true for all government assistance programs, whether the programs be for the people at the bottom tiers of the pyramid or the ones at the top. **Once the spigot of low-cost low-accountability capital is turned on, it will be difficult to turn it off.** Turn it off and face the wrath of the newly offended class of individuals. Don't follow through on the original time-limited scale of assistance and run the risk of losing all credibility.

Does Lowering Taxes Stimulate the Economy?

The premise behind this argument is that when the financial burden on a business is reduced, then it leaves more money on the table for the business to put to better use. Given that businesses in general are looking for ways and means to improve their return on investments, the additional wealth would therefore be put to use in either expanding the business, hiring new employees, or making other investments that would make the business more profitable. If all of these were true, then it would obviously result in greater productivity, higher employment, and as a whole, a boon for the economy.

From business owners' perspective, this is pure fiction. For example, if a particular business is earning the owner $100K, for instance, and the taxation on that is $25K, he/she gets to keep the remaining $75K. Here the taxation rate is a flat 25 percent. If the government were to reduce the taxation to 10 percent, then this individual would have an additional $15K. Given that no other changes are anticipated vis-à-vis the business itself, what motivation is there for the owner to plow this money back into the business? On the contrary, will that money not end up in his/her own personal account or investments?

Alternatively, if the business is growing and getting busier, and everyone is gainfully employed to the maximum, there is further prospect for growth to continue; however, in order to absorb more business orders, there is a need to expand the work force. Failure to increase the work force will reflect in the capacity to deliver services and goods in a timely and qualitative manner. In this scenario, if the taxation were to change from 25 percent to 35 percent, would that impede any employment decisions? The answer is most likely not unless the business profit margin is so small that the additional taxation would wipe out any margin.

Likewise, if the economy is going through a rough patch and the prospect of any growth in business environments is scant, lowering taxation to even 5 percent will not be enough to stimulate any hiring because it still doesn't change the basic business environment. If, on the other hand, the government decides to pump capital into the lower rungs of the pyramid, either through tax breaks or lowered interest on personal borrowing or assistance checks to people, this would stimulate the innate consumption trends that are part and parcel of normal living. This, in turn, would force the capital to exchange hands among the people, even if in small quantities. This would eventually result in some of that capital ending up on the door-step of the very businesses that are experiencing a slowdown. If enough business end up in this position, then this might produce the conditions that warrant the need for an increase in the labor force, hence initiating the hiring cycle. **Nothing hurts a recovery from a slowdown more than a mismatch between the consumption needs of the people and the inavailability of capital among the same people.**

What Will Work in a Recessionary Economy—Austerity versus Stimulation

When economic activity begins to slow down, what needs to be done? The intuitive answer is to cut spending. If the inflow of money into the coffers is drying up, then it makes sense to make adjustments to the outflow. "You don't spend what you don't have!" Most people use simplistic home finance management rules to explain the need to cut spending. Does it really work?

Let's go back to the original model of the economy being an engine where the capital (money) is the fuel running through the engine. Economic activity does not exist to increase the money in the system; rather, the money flow exists to keep the economy running. The economy provides the value and the context for the money. As long as there is an unimpeded flow of money through the entire system, economic activity does not drop beyond a certain minimum level. This is the level of innate economic activity that results from the simple acts of normal living. Every human living in the system has consumption needs to meet their existential requirements of food, clothing, residence, transportation, health, schooling, child care, etc. No matter what happens to the rest of the world, every one of these individuals is going to try to find some way of meeting these minimum essential needs. This is the innate minimum latent consumption pattern of the population. But in order for individuals to be able to conclude each one of these transactions, they need to have the ability to get some money, either their own or the money they obtain through lending or through government safety net programs. If they cannot gain access to any funds, then they will begin to cut back on the essentials, and that in turn will reduce the minimum consumption from these tiers even more.

In this environment, if austerity measures are implemented, then this results in the drying up of capital availability to sections of the population that are dependent on help to continue to consume. In turn, this will have a greater cooling effect on economic activity. With the reduction of capital exchanging hands in the lower tiers, there is even less capital available to move up the pyramid. This decrease in the amount of capital in the pyramid results in progressively negative business forecasts among the higher tiers, and these businesses would be less likely to risk contributing to prodding the economy by offering any increase in hiring. This impasse has no way of self-correcting itself, as any decision within the austerity logic results in perpetuating the downward spiral.

It is understandable that the natural reaction to the government handing out money to the lower tiers of society is that it is wasteful, that it rewards the maintenance of status quo, and that it provides a disincentive for people to get a job. This viewpoint might be right. The practice of providing government support to the financially weak, especially during an economic downturn, is meant to take place for only a limited amount of time, and it is not meant to continue into perpetuity. Failure to be disciplined about maintaining the timeliness of the assistance is a manifestation of human nature rather than the error of the logic behind it. With government assistance going to the lower tiers of the pyramid, the basic minimum consumption patterns for subsistence are maintained. This in turn allows for capital turnover, continuing, albeit, at a slower pace. Furthermore, the capital that is introduced at the bottom of the pyramid invariably almost immediately leaves the hands of its primary recipients through consumption spending. There is hardly any potential for hoarding of the capital. This is, therefore, a very predictable way of ensuring that the money flow within the system will continue unimpeded.

If the same wealth were to be introduced at the top of the pyramid, two obvious differences would be noted. First, the pool of the recipients would be smaller, and the individual handout would be much larger. Second, there would be a greater risk of the capital being hoarded than it being utilized immediately. This in turn would cause the equivalent effect of flight of capital from the system. While stimulation during a downturn might be prudent, it would also be most effective when administered to the sections of the pyramid where utilization of the funds is assured to be immediate. Furthermore, the capital that is released in the bottom tiers will eventually climb up the pyramid.

The fear of the opposite happening, where the funds provided would contribute to establishment of long-term dysfunctional behavior in the recipient class of people, is a valid one. What if the "free money" made available to these tiers of society was used to promote and maintain illegal activities such as drug use and alcoholism, which in turn promotes vagrant and delinquent behavior? This would result in destructive processes that would add to the financial burden of the system. Instead of the money stimulating capital churn through the system, it might catalyze the destructive elements. This is an easily avoidable predicament as this is the result of the lack of disciplined management of the "stimulus process," which in turn is the result of poor public auditing and transparency and lack of a coherent strategy.

While stimulating an economy by pumping money into the structure or cutting down on government services through austerity measures are meant to only apply brakes to the downward spiral of an economy, these measures by themselves will not reverse the conditions that brought on the economic downturn in the first place. The actual turnaround to a status of health requires the engine returning to normal running at all levels.

And this brings up the question: What makes a running economy spiral out of control and begin the process of slowing down? This is simplistically interpreted within the engine-fuel analogy. To reiterate, if the economy is represented by a running engine, the fuel that runs the engine is the money or capital flowing through the engine. The efficient, continuous circulation of capital through the entire system ensures continuous optimal functioning of the economy. **The capital accumulation in the hands of the few is an offshoot of a functioning economy and not the reason for the economic activity**. The function of a well-running economy is to be productive, where products and services are made and delivered to points of consumption. The intrinsic value of these services and products is realized when it is tabulated using a quantifiable mechanism like money. In other words, by itself, money has no intrinsic value; its value is reflected in its ability to establish the intrinsic value of goods and services being transacted. If the economy tanks, the value of the money falls; if the economy is healthy, then the money's value appreciates. This means that it is not the absolute quantity of money or capital accumulated that determines the statuses of being well off or poor, but rather what the purchasing power of that capital is. Even though money has only a reflective value, it, because of its capacity to transact exchanges within the system, acquires, by assignment, a value that makes it worthy of being hoarded. This causes the capital to become pooled in sections of the system. When capital gets pooled, it becomes unavailable for circulation, and within the engine-fuel analogy this means that there is less fuel in the lines to keep the engine running smoothly. This in turn might lead to the engine slowing down or becoming less efficient, which inadvertently influences the value of the money. **Saving money might be good economic planning at the individual level, but it is bad for the system if done to an extreme.**

The other reason the economic engine might have issues is **flight of capital from the system**. The global economy consists of many independently run economic systems. Each system, in addition to serving its resident population's consumption requirements, also tries to facilitate other systems' requirements competitively. If other economic zones offer a more lucrative labor rate, it is tempting to a business to consider relocating its labor source to these cheaper zones. One of the ways to recirculate capital within the system is to fund employment within the system. If instead labor is getting outsourced, then there is a reduction of employment at home, which means there is less capital circulation in the system. Furthermore, as this decision to move labor out is based on an increase expected in the profit margin and its resultant higher-retained capital within the business structure, this would further reduce the recirculation of capital through the system. This policy is not the result of sound long-term economic planning but rather plain and simple *greed*. Ironically, this scheme of things results in some businesses becoming financially successful in the short run, but eventually in the long term the lack of capital within the home system causes the economy to slow down, resulting in reduction in productivity, which then comes back to bite the very businesses that profited originally. This starts a new cycle of self-cannibalization to keep the profit margins up. If the money inflow is adversely affected due to reduction in productivity and consumption, then the only adjustment that can be made is to reduce the outflow of money through overhead and expense modifications. The businesses begin reducing the biggest source of overheads (i.e., employees) that in turn aggravates the downward spiral. **Valuing profit making at the expense of the health of the economy is a winner-less process in the long run.**

Outsourcing Labor—Boon or Benefit on the Whole?

In the earlier section, it was concluded that outsourcing labor is unhealthy for one's own economy. However, if the world is considered to consist of multiple autonomous economic engines functioning and interacting with each other, it becomes difficult to not be exposed to competitive pressures of material cost, manufacturing, labor, etc. It would be unrealistic to try and clamp down on businesses, preventing them from choosing to utilize the less expensive options as a way of managing their overhead costs. In the interaction of economies, the fundamental principle of prevention of flight of capital can still be made to work. **Labor that leaves an economic zone for identical quality labor at a cheaper rate is essentially labor that is no longer sustainable within the current economic structure.** This is a natural offshoot of the evolution of the economy. All economies go through a similar growth pattern. In the early days of any nation, the economy is largely agrarian with very little manufacturing. It consists of populations that work at a very inexpensive labor rate, and consumption requirements are very basic: food, clothing, shelter, schooling, and basic transportation. As the country develops and the economy matures, the same basic requirements are made more complex. More urban areas begin to from. Rural areas become delineated as the food-producing areas and the urban areas become more consumption-heavy areas. Employment patterns change with the addition of manufacturing and service-sector jobs. Pay scales tip in favor of the manufacturing and service-sector jobs, forcing people to opt out of farming types of labor. This inevitably is accompanied by a population shift toward the urban areas. Cities and townships grow in size, and along with this growth the cost of developing and maintaining the infrastructure to connect and serve the population becomes more complex and expensive. In the past, while people could have walked to most places of interest, now they become dependent on mass transit or personal modes of transportation. Since the food production zones are located farther away, it then becomes necessary to transport and house products in large supermarkets to meet the needs of the urban population. Density of the population in the urban areas brings with it the challenges of safe housing, safe water supply, and safe waste disposal. In other words, as the economic zone evolves, it also becomes more complex. With complexity comes increased manpower utilization for the same tasks, hence these tasks begin to become more expensive. For example, housing and food prices begin to rise. This in turn makes labor even more in demand and expensive. If at this point the country is wealthy enough to offshore its food production requirements to another developing nation, then it will begin to continue to see a shift in employment away from the rural sectors to the more industry and urban sectors. For this economy to operate under a rural-heavy focus would be detrimental. The loss of rural jobs is an evolutionary trend that can be offset by adequate planning to increase capital inflow into the economic zone by selling the manufacturing and service products back to the lesser-developed zone. However, this needs to be done in an orderly fashion, or else it the situation will eventually become chaotic with a lot of collateral damage and pain and strife for the affected employed population. This kind of planning is the result of having the right kind of people at the helm, be it an industry or a political apparatus entrusted to make the accurate forecast and prepare the nation for it. This also means that trade among different economic zones has to be neutral in value to the inherent capital within any given system. **Development of any one economic zone at the expense of another zone will be detrimental to the entire fabric of intereconomy interaction.**

In other words, if during this interaction between two or more economies any one of them, due to economic mismanagement or to the ability to possess a better economy, attempts to manipulate the process in its favor, this will result in one of the economies losing its inherent capital. This will cause the economy to spiral downward even more. The richer economies might get wealthier from this interaction, but they will eventually pay a price by having to deal with the dysfunctional economy of the poorer nation. The richer economy will end up having to subsidize the mismanagement to prevent it from a total collapse, or it will have to deal with the consequences of mismanagement in the form of wars, piracy, and criminal enterprise establishment, all of which will undercut the benefits of the profits generated earlier. **Rather than competitive development, competitive codevelopment is more sustainable.** Within the codevelopment model, the loss of capital through loss of one type of labor will be compensated by the return of other types of employment for which the nation's population and economy would be better suited. Until now, the evolutionary pattern in maturing economies has been one that follows the following pattern: agrarian to industrial manufacturing to service-heavy to information-heavy economies. When the population is sufficiently prepared in advance for such changes, the economies will continue to develop in an upward manner. When economies fail to anticipate such changes and challenge their inherent labor force to retrain for newer prospects, this is when the economy falters and becomes vulnerable to external factors.

How Can a Correction of Labor Rate Inequities Take Place?

The reason jobs leave an economy for another is because of more competitive labor rates, among many other factors. What establishes the labor rate of an economic zone?

To some extent, the minimum is established by a government decree or law. How does one still determine the labor rate? It is the rate at which someone would be willing to do a job. Why is it then a plumber charges forty to eight dollars minimum for making a trip to an address while the same job might be done in, say, for example, China for probably two dollars. Why this large a discrepancy in cost? When you have individual, isolated economy zones with minimal to no interlinking, the labor rate is essentially determined by what the market sets as being a fair and competitive price. The plumber in question, for example, can demand a fee of zero to one hundred dollars. The market will respond favorably to the rate at a certain level and below. Determining this rate is the hard part, but it is largely based on supply and demand, skill set proficiency, availability, and also the presence or absence of competition. The problem arises when previously isolated job pools become capable of easily relocating in the global market. Now they become subject to market forces and to rates on a global scale. If, hypothetically, Chinese plumbers had access to and could service house calls in the United States, the labor rate of plumbers' house calls would dramatically fall. The two ways of dealing with competitive labor rate are to either a) accept that the competition is a harbinger of necessary change to be implemented and retrain the work force for other forms of labor or b) figure out a way to compete without losing the ability to affect significant lifestyle change.

How can a first-world economy compete with a developing economy on the labor rate?

Let's begin by setting the labor rate arbitrarily to be competitive and then work from there to figure out what else needs to happen in order for the work force to able to thrive with this new labor rate and still continue to maintain an undepreciated lifestyle. Continuing with the plumber example, let's assume the plumber in question makes approximately $30,000 and uses that income to support his/her family by providing the means to housing, food, clothing, schooling, child care, etc. This is all done by maintaining an industry labor rate of forty-five dollars per hour. Of this, the personal labor rate is fifteen dollars and 0.625 cents per hour (wage rate). Obviously at this low pay scale, there is minimal prospect of any money being left over for savings. A plumber in China or India might be able to provide *similar services with training* for about ten dollars per hour; however, when that rate enters the global pool, it will be adjusted to a more equitable rate of maybe twenty-five dollars per hour because it needs to take into the account the many layers of intermediating agencies and personnel that will indirectly get involved to regulate it. In order to compete, the US plumber does not really have to match or beat the twenty-five-dollar labor rate because at twenty-five dollars the service is still being rendered by an outside agency with little or no local standing, and furthermore with no known history of reliability. The US agency can provide that level of comfort of acquaintance, reliability, and local origination and thereby proclaim a better-responsive client management. For that the agency will be forgiven for charging a bit more. But the plumber might have to be ready to provide his or her services at a competitive rate of, say, thirty dollars per hour.

Now the big question is how can an existing business, functioning within its current business environment with all its rules, regulations, and constraints, offer its services at a one-third discount and still keep its profit margin?

Labor Rate

Every product and service in an economy has a price assigned to it. The basic formula for that price is Material Cost + Energy Cost + Labor Cost + Profit Margin + Taxation Rate + Reserve Buffer. This total is then weighed against the demand that exists, combined with the presence or absence of competitors, and then a final market-sustainable price is set. High demand in combination with no competition leads to monopolistic price fixing with a resultant huge profit margin. (This high profit eventually bleeds into the employee pool, and in turn employees become accustomed to higher wage benefits, which translates into an uptick in the innate labor rate within the organization.) Every material destined for some product or service that enters the nation goes through a series of handlings, each of which ends up in adding to the cost of the product. For example, in the price of peanut oil, the cost modification begins right from the point of procurement. The first price fixed is that by the farmer to a wholesaler. The wholesaler through transportation and storage and later distribution adds on its cost to the product. The peanuts then arrive at the factory for processing and extraction of oil. The factor then adds its cost to the product. The peanut oil then gets stored again and transported to various facilities that are entrusted with its final sale. These facilities now tack on their own cost to the peanut oil. At each of these levels, in addition to acquisition cost, the add-ons take in to account energy, storage overhead, labor costs, and finally profit before passing the product on to next handler. In all of these levels, if the labor cost is forcibly or arbitrarily pegged to a low rate, this will then exert its influence on the final pricing by a reverse multiplier effect. So theoretically, the price of products can be scaled down dramatically just by holding the labor rate down. The other component that needs to be regulated and controlled is the profit margin that is tacked on the over-head price. Greed control is vital to prevent prices from remaining at their current levels, even after labor-rate modifications are implemented, as this will result in unsustainable profit margins and a market collapse. The percentage of profit can be maintained even if the price of products is adjusted downward. In this scenario, it is not the de-evaluation of the money but rather an increase in its purchasing power without any correction to the international intercurrency arrangements. Thus, it is theoretically possible to reset the internal labor rate of the nation to be competitive with the outside world. This has immense implication to the economy in the long run.

One of the most endearing reasons for offshore business displacement is the favorable labor cost availability. If the labor cost at home is pegged to a competitive rate, then there would be fewer reasons for flight of businesses from the national economic zone. For example, a factory worker in China working in an enterprise like Foxconn, making appliances for the United States and the rest of world, gets paid approximately $300 per month (2011 statistic). The equivalent worker force employee in the United States is paid approximately $3,000 per month. If the labor rate for the same employee was to be arbitrarily set at $1,000 per month, it would have rippling ramification throughout the system. On the face of it, it appears that by setting the wage to one-third of the original wage we are assuredly pushing the employee into poverty, and yes, that would be true if everything else around the employee didn't reflect the downward pressure in pricing. If wages are set lower, then this means that the overhead cost of labor for that product has gone down by significantly. If similar labor cost resetting is done at every enterprise across the land in a planned and programmed manner, this would lead to a reduction in the cost of goods and services across the board. Since the labor rate plays into the pricing of any commodity multiple times depending on the number of times the product has passed through the various handling stages before being sold, the labor rate correction would have a price-reducing effect at all of these stages. It would also have an effect on the energy component of the overhead, as energy too has labor cost figuring into it through the various stages of handling from the point of energy extraction to the point of distribution. The parts of the overhead that need a concerted effort to rectify are the profit margin and taxation, which are largely autonomous to market force manipulations like that of the labor rate. However, the overriding question is whether a correction to the labor rate, as in this example of a reduction of cost by about two-thirds, is sufficient to entice businesses to retain their operations within the country? If not, at what point will the local labor rate be favorable to prevent flight of businesses, and secondly, is it even possible to achieve that low a competitive rate by manipulation? Finally, in this new reality, will the price correction of all commodities help the lifestyle-maintaining cost of living to keep pace with the reduction of the wage amount? Theoretically, by reducing the wage and resetting the cost of living downward, the lifestyle should not be any more different than it was before. This, of course, would be the ideal conclusion. It makes sense to manipulate the wage rate and peg it to a globally competitive rate because there will always be cheaper competition available. Today this competition comes from countries like China and India. Tomorrow it could be from Sub-Saharan countries. The alternative is to constantly retrain the working population to deal with evermore increasingly sophisticated types of skill sets. Either way requires a planned and coordinated approach utilizing collaboration between government and business enterprises.

If the labor rate correction results in a downward adjustment in the cost of living without a loss of lifestyle, then why is it that, despite salaries across the board being either stagnant or declining over the last two decades, the cost of living has continued to rise?

There are other measures that need to be instituted along with resetting the labor rate to put downward pressure on the cost of living. No business will willingly reset their product pricing lower just because the cost of manufacturing becomes less expensive. The nature of the business is to maximize its profits. If wages are set lower without exerting any pressure on the businesses to reflect the new cost in product pricing, then the businesses will just reap higher profits, and this will ensure a widening gulf between the rich and the poor. The government would have to get involved in the unpleasant business of helping determine the maximum allowable price of different commodities, ensuring that the profit taking is also regulated and not egregious, and finally instituting some form reward measures to incentivize reinvestment of profits into the businesses themselves, in personal development and skill enhancements, rather than allowing the profits to be paid out as executive bonuses, which would then result in flight of capital. That would also mean capping executive pays to a reasonable level within a competitive range of international pay scales for similar positions and responsibility. **Unchecked greed is destructive to the system while focused and harnessed ambitious endeavors might be very beneficial for development.** Is there political will and stamina to explore, let alone institute, any of these options? Doubtful.

How about the alternative? Consider the proposal that has been around for a while to raise the minimum wage to standards considered worthy of a developed nation. In the absence of regulating the labor rate in the nation to a competitive level with the outside market zones, raising the labor rate at the minimum wage end makes sense. Any wage increase at the minimum wage end will, in essence, be an economic stimulus package delivered to the people who will most likely put it to use in consumption-driven activities. The important difference is that this stimulus be given to the employed people instead of the alternative government dole. Though individual businesses may complain about how this affects their bottom line, in reality it has the prospect of improving their bottom line in the long run. (The government could help the businesses by lowering the payroll taxes. Thus, increased money gets distributed to more of the employed with a reduced tax penalty to the business.) The increased availability of money will lead to higher consumption activities, which in turn will allow the money to circulate upward, and eventually it will register by an uptick of business activity for the very same business that initially felt the increase was burdensome. Businesses spend money to bring increased traffic to their doorstep is called marketing, but there is no guarantee of promised results. Increased wages at any level increases spending habits, and that will always be a business booster rather than a business killer.

The other peculiarity with low-wage jobs is that they are less likely to be exported to less expensive economic zones, as these are mostly local employment jobs.

There is, however, a ripple effect that might have negative ramifications, in the short run at least. For example, if we were to raise the minimum wage to a hypothetical twelve dollars per hour, this would mean that everyone who is employed, irrespective of skill or experience level, would have to be paid this minimum wage. Currently in the dental field in Southern California, dental assistants at entry level earn at the wage rate of approximately ten to twelve dollars per hour on average. If the minimum wage of twelve dollars per hour gets you an inexperienced employee, then wouldn't the experienced employees in fields like the dental industry expect to be paid more? If the wages of dental assistants are upgraded, then automatically it follows that all the other wages in the business will need to be readjusted upward as well (i.e., all except the owners, because that is where the reduction in wages will need to be considered to keep the overheads in check). The employers who agree to the minimum wage are voicing their disapproval in large part because of this feared uptick in overhead through salary increases. However, if they are mandated to follow through in providing this wage, then most employers will be hanging on to the hope that the promise of increased business activity as a result of this employer-sourced economic stimulus will come to fruition and help offset the increase in overhead with increase in revenue.

Increasing minimum wage has another ripple effect. Since the 1970s wage disparity has been increasing every year. The American dream of well-paying employment has all but disappeared for most people except for those at the very top in any industry. The wage spread, the gulf between the least-paid employee and the CEO, has been increasing. One of the signs by which the health of an economy is truly measured is in this wealth spread. Ideally, the spread should be as narrow as possible. By instituting a minimum wage of, say, a "generous" twenty dollars per hour, there will no doubt be an uptick in the salaries of all above the minimum wage category. This uptick will begin to diminish as people climb through the middle management tiers as they will encounter a reactive pushback from the top to hold the salaries within a reasonable range or risk getting pushed out competitively by other job zones. This combination of the upward effect of raising the minimum wage with the downward pressure from higher management to contain the runaway salary inflation will cause the wage spread to shrink and stabilize to a level that will become sustainable for the economy, at least in the short run.

Raising the minimum wage can have other positive ripple effects. A wealthier lower class of wage earners is bound to be made up of more confident consumers. If these wage earners are certain of earning more than the bare minimum, then they know that they can take risks in life in terms of self-employment options, investments, and home ownership. They might actually attempt to fulfill their desires of shoring up educational priorities, healthcare needs, healthy lifestyle choices, etc. They can even allocate a portion of the money for nonconsumption items in the form of savings. This might in turn reduce their dependence on government dole or government retirement funds, which in turn will free up the government from worrying about bankrupting government programs. All of this is the best-case scenario. The worst is that the bad habits people have gotten used to in the past decades will continue.

Low wage earners will continue to subsist paycheck to paycheck with no effort applied to altering their spending patterns, leading to unhealthier, government-dependent lifestyles. While there might be some outliers, the vast majority of the earners will respond by taking some positive measures to put their lives in order. Hardship can be a forceful teacher.

Greed Is Good—Really?

This is the motto behind American economic success. Is it really a motivator for economic success, or is it merely a delusionary concept that provides short-term financial gain while ignoring the accumulation of structural flaws in the system due to taking shortcuts. In any enterprise there is a right way of doing things and a wrong way of doing things. The right and wrong is based not on moral principles but rather on the effect either leaves behind. If a particular action, no matter how beneficial it is for the few, leaves in its wake deleterious side effects for the majority, then it cannot be justified even if the action has no explicit illegality attached to it. Legality or lack of it is a very low bar to try and jump over.

In an unregulated environment, the logic behind market forces is challenging one entity's performance against another. In that performance, the element of personal greed becomes inherent to the process, and the competition becomes one of destructive success. For one entity to attain success, it has to be at the behest of the failure of another. But what is lost in this kind of market functioning is that a lot of individuals who are aligned to the workings of a company, through no fault of their own, become subject to the negative consequences of a destructive market environment. The justification for having the "strongest eat the weakest" comes from the Darwinian philosophy of how things function in the wild natural existence—survival of the fittest. Human endeavors need to rise above the basic constructs of this Darwinian point of view. Either that, or we should not be paying even a lip service to the ideas of fairness and helping the unfortunate because they run contrary to the Darwinian concept of survival.

It is precisely to prevent such catastrophic consequences to lack of control in the market that government intervention, through establishing regulation to monitor and at times intervene, becomes necessary. However, even within this regulated environment, monopolies have been allowed to thrive. Monopolistic endeavors are even more egregious in the pursuance of greed-based services. Monopolies do not have to even compete with any other entity, and hence can set the rules of engagement with their customers without any sense of fairness. While they do operate in a government-regulated environment, monopolies are allowed to noncompetitively set the terms of service contracts with their customers. In this environment, greed poisons the relationship of the monopoly with its customer base and eventually results in a backlash that will cost the very same company to lose market share. This in turn results in the company indulging in cost cutting by laying off the very same workers who helped create the company in the first place. This is another consequence of the destructive market environment. The monopolistic company did benefit for a short period of time, but in the long run its behavior proved quite detrimental.

What is greed, and how is it different from ambition? Ambition usually leads a person to remain competitive in trying to qualitatively improve himself or herself with regard to a specific parameter, and in doing so, to attain a particular rewarding position in life. The parameter might be wealth, expertise, position of power, etc. Greed, on the other hand, is more focused on the final goal and attaining it by any means necessary without necessarily having to be qualitatively improved. More often than not, the parameter is financial reward. Ambition is focused, goal-centered, and effort-modulated action. Greed is an opportunistic wealth-hoarding enterprise. Ambition may or may not be coupled with unscrupulousness, but greed is definitely accompanied by unscrupulous behavior.

seven

Concept of History

This thought originally occurred to me after the events of 9/11. At that time a lot of soul-searching was being conducted at the individual level and at the larger national level. One of the common thought trends that made its way into the public domain through the various medias was the concept of "the ugly American," the brash, self-centered American who will have his or her way in world affairs irrespective of how many nations have to be insulted or stepped on to reach the end goals. On the other end of the spectrum was this sense of disbelief, especially among Americans, that nothing America had done was deserving of this kind of negative attention. One group of people rejoiced or at least agreed that the attacks were consequential to past American behavior and that they were a sort of just comeuppance. Others were shocked out of their complacency and belief that being geographically distant and isolated from the hot spots of the world would render them immune to the effects of instabilities and chaos among other nations. As an immigrant myself, the part that I found missing or lost in the discourse was the idea of what was the consensus concept of history and the impact of historical behavior. The mismatch in the perception was that what was perceived as being of historical importance to the rest of the world was somehow being dismissed as not having any relevance within the United States.

History is an interpretation of incidents that have happened. Since we do not possess the foresight to document with great veracity and accuracy the details of events as they unfold, we are dependent on collecting the vast array of subjective viewpoints and eyewitness accounts in order to stitch together the closest narrative of events long gone by. This effort is further compromised by the biases held by the compilers of the narrative. Hence, history, or the perception of historical events, can never truly be considered error free and absolutely factual. If history is a matter of interpretation, then the sense of history among people is based on the successful retelling of that compelling narrative.

Why is it that sense of history is perceived differently in the United States as compared to the rest of the world, or is it? Perception of history rests on three legs. Leg One: Commemorative history where incidents are remembered by celebration events. Leg Two: In-memoriam history involving anniversaries of the traumatic incidents in question. Leg Three: Grievances history involving perceived grievances of foreign influences. In the first case of commemorative history, the celebratory nature of remembrance becomes ingrained in the cultural folklore and becomes a quaint characteristic of that particular culture. In the United States, for example, there are different reenactments of Civil War battles that are done yearly to remember the historical relevance of a particular place. These are usually fun-filled events that combine a history reminder with family gatherings. The in-memoriam history involves the more somber retelling of horrific moments—for example, the attack on Pearl Harbor or the assassination of JFK. This is usually done with the idea of encouraging introspection and reflection. Grievances history is the result of multigenerational reverberations of traumatic events, like wars, conflicts, and suffering under despotic rule.

Particularly under wars and conflicts, there is a destruction of identities—religious, cultural, or otherwise—that tends to have a lasting impact on the national psyche. This destruction threatens the perception of self and the collective sense of community identity. Society exists on account of the interwoven nature of individual identities, egos, and aspirations within a historical context of coexistence. This sense is further bonded by community affiliations to religious, political, and cultural institutions and common experiences that have shaped societal norms. In conflicts this fabric is shredded, and in the process, it releases many echoes of individual experiences of trauma, which resonate for a considerable time and sometimes well into the next generation. Globally there is hardly any nation that has not had to suffer the consequences of a war or an invasion.

Until recently, the memories of these traumas have been allowed to be washed away by the cleansing act of time. While there are some cultural remnants of past conflicts still lingering in most societies, people have by and large learned to move past them and erase them from their immediate memory. The memories of these horrendous conflicts have become relegated, as they should be, to the pages of historical texts or to anniversary celebratory events. No mourning-filled reminders or jingoistic propagandas of past conflicts have been perpetuated within the societies, and hence in time these events have become forgotten. Awareness of one's history is not the same as constantly reliving one's history, especially when the focus is always on the suffering. Individuals' health and pride stems from knowing who they are, within a historical context, without being subject to the negative burdens of past indiscretions or a sense of victimhood that is endlessly being perpetuated.

In this modern era, however, those old rules have undergone a dramatic change. We now have the ability to record wars and conflicts in great detail and in vivid resolution. Now we can indefinitely revisit the original traumas of conflict from the comforts of an armchair. If society is not allowed to forget, then it cannot be in a position to heal itself. It can repeatedly inflict upon itself the psychic trauma, and thereby perpetuate the sense of being under assault or under the threat of imminent destruction. In the modern era, due to the ability to record events for posterity, these events have attained a life span unlike any other events in the past. This is of some importance in the discussion.

In the past, any traumatic event, such as the death of an individual at the hands of another, would have resulted in a sense of outrage and the need for justice or revenge accumulating from within that victim's immediate family. That sense could be perpetuated within the family even without any recordings. Word-of-mouth transference of the event will suffice to continue to propagate the sense of outrage, even through multiple generations. In a society, however, such transference of combined trauma can only be perpetuated as a result of a systematic propaganda-style retelling of the incident. It is no surprise that nations that do not have the capacity to reinvent themselves and reinvigorate themselves are the ones where the perpetuation of the slights and insults of these conflicts is easily managed. Coincidentally, these are also the societies that have a lot of built-in dysfunction. These are societies that have to deal with inept and inefficient governments, corrupt institutions, and poverty, and they have large numbers of unemployed and suffer from sectarian strains on the basis of differences in religious practices or feudal makeup. In these societies, the memories of insults perpetuated through conflicts can be kept alive and festering for a long time as they serve to deflect the population's attention from the immediate obvious shortcomings of their ruling class.

Ironically, in nations under despotic rule, the dynamics are a little different. For all the grievances perpetuated by a despotic regime on its citizens, because it is a constant and relatively chronic-grade enforcement, people generally tend to get "acclimatized" to this environment and then to forget about the alternate possibilities. However, if the same nation were to be attacked or subjected to an externally motivated violent change, then the resultant trauma would be one that would be attributed to foreign involvement. Sadly, this makes absolute sense. Even in the worst conditions under despotic rule, the rules of existence are perfectly clear, and to some extent predictable. The society had woven its fabric of coexistence within that framework. Imperfect as it might have been, that framework was still the norm. Change, on the other hand, is a violent upheaval of the norm, and it comes with a price. The price is traumatic, and in a decimated society, the agent of change becomes the focus of blame, and the resultant trauma is then associated with the agent of the change.

Why is all of this pertinent to what the average American feels or needs to feel? American influence around the world, particularly after the Second World War, has been extremely penetrating and effective. Admittedly, this influence is geared toward protecting and furthering American security interests and economic interests. It might be a matter of debate internally whether the policies being pursued are actually at the behest of large corporate entities rather than being the nation's interests, but internationally these policies are all perceived as American interests. To the rest of the world, the ownership of the consequences of any American involvement rests with the entire population of the United States of America. So while on one hand American money might subsidize infrastructure construction or food aid, on the other hand it might also be perceived as being responsible in propping up a corrupt despot. The association of the American influence to the act is more likely to be remembered when it results in negative outcomes more than positive outcomes. So while American dollars subsidize the social hand-out and provide food and shelter aid to the poor in countries like the Saudi Kingdom or Yemen, their military associations and arms sales to the kingdom help to keep the despotic regimes in control. Americans might allude to social aid as being an example of an effort to promote the American brand, but the people of the despotic regimes are more likely to say that the inability to change a brutal and unfair regime is due to the monetary and military support the regime receives from the United States. These perceived grievances will become part of the historical folklore in some quarters, and this will then be the fuel that feeds conspiracy-spouting anarchist criminal enterprises.

Assigning blame based on the effects of either wars or propped-up despotic rulers is aimed at the entire nation of the United States. Irrespective of whether individuals may or may not have personally supported the "egregious" policies, as citizens of the nation every single American is considered to be equally responsible. (*This is one of the primary reasons for the citizens of this nation to participate more actively in auditing the functioning of their government. It would also help if they could cultivate a sense of cynicism toward their elected representatives and demand a more open and mature reporting of their accomplishments. Unchained and unchecked, any government enterprise can become opaque and defiant to any need to report back to their citizen constituents the true workings of their agencies. The splitting of the population into the right and left ideological boxes makes it convenient for the powers that be to obfuscate and confuse the population about their actual work. Every action this nation undertakes, good or bad, is at the behest of its citizens. In other words, the ultimate responsibility rests not just with any particular administration, but with the nation in particular and with its citizens as a whole.*) You might not have supported any of the past war efforts, but because you are a citizen of this nation, you are just as responsible for the war's effect as the ones who supported them. That is the price of citizenship. It is true that this equation of extended responsibility to every citizen is valid for any nation. However, unlike other nations, America is unique in its influence and capacity to be able to make or break countries' economies with some ease. While the average citizen is blissfully unaware of the actions of their own government in other nations, the citizens of those nations are made aware of these negative American actions either through personal experience or through the retelling of the actions by other agencies. The most recent example of American action that incites anger toward the nation is the use of drones to hunt criminal elements. The average American is really not aware of the effect this policy has other than through the sterilized reporting that sometimes surfaces in the media. But for most citizens who have to bear the brunt of the attacks, especially when there is significant collateral damage, they have no difficulty in assigning the blame to the entire citizenry of the country. Imagine an entire population nursing a personal grudge against the United States because of the effects of the drone campaign. These people do not need the help of any propaganda-style remembrances, as they can feel the effect of this drone campaign and relive it in their minds for years to come. This memory becomes a part of their ever-present reality. Even after the American nation has moved on, the citizens of these other nations will hold fast to the memories and repeat the stories of these horrors into perpetuity. For them, these incidents will never be relegated to the realms of histories of the past.

Can people ever move past the horrors of yesteryears? Apparently yes, and with some ease too. A classic example of a nation that seems to have put the horrors behind them is Vietnam. For all that the population of Vietnam had to endure through the years of war, one would expect its citizens to still be nursing a grudge against the United States. But the Vietnamese seem to have forgiven, if not forgotten, the horrors of that war. Is it because of a cultural difference? Maybe, but it is also because after the Vietnam War ended, American influence has waned in that part of the world, especially since the dynamics of cold war have changed too. Therefore, absent any perception of interference by the citizens of Vietnam on the part of the US government and some liberalization of economic policies, the nation has gotten busy with economic rebirth and growth. Their current reality finds them with an improved status, and this allows for the effects of time to play out naturally. The Vietnamese have learned to forget and perhaps forgive.

Lack of historical appreciation among the citizens of the United States is because, contrastingly, Americans are not aware of the destructive ripples their foreign policies have had on many of these nations. Devoid of traumatic experiences, there is no reason to become sensitive to the effects of one's actions. In the modern era, America has been fortunate in enjoying an extended period of relative stability. Even through the world wars and the subsequent Vietnam and Korean conflicts and all of the other small and medium battles, the nation of the United States has not come under attack, except for Pearl Harbor. Having not encountered firsthand the effects of the conflicts right in their own hometowns and backyards, American citizens cannot understand the debilitating effects of violence, especially the kind that only a war can produce. Despite sending its citizens to fight in distant lands, the United States has never had to suffer the ignominy of being invaded or being subject to occupation. Therefore, for US citizens, there are no communal or societal memories of the trauma of battle. There are no communal emotional scars from destroyed hometowns to contend with. This is why the 9/11 attacks were so traumatic to the nation even though the impact area was limited to a few city blocks in two different cities and the number dead was less than five thousand. By comparison, most other nations that have blamed American handiwork, directly or indirectly, in their fight against terrorists or insurgencies see their causalities numbering in the tens or hundreds of thousands. In these interactions, the trauma accumulates in some other nation while the average American is blissfully unaware of any effects his or her nation has on the rest of the world. The other irony is that the attacks that are now being directed against the American interest are being conducted by people formerly trained and armed by Americans themselves. The tragic irony of this is more apparent to citizens of other nations than to Americans themselves.

The other pertinent question to ask would be that if the US influence across the globe results in animosity toward the United States, then how is it that the United States has not had to deal with similar attacks like the 9/11 attack originating more frequently from other groups in the world? Since the United States has been attacked on its own soil only twice in a century, maybe it is not an ideal example to use to show the global cause-and-effect relationship of American policies. However, this discussion is more on the concept of history and how it might explain the justification used for the antagonistic attitudes that Americans face in some quarters of the world. Yet, ironically this anti-Americanism exists only as a response to the continuation of American influence-peddling. When and if America decides to withdraw completely its huge footprint from these nations, the animosity will peter out in time. But can the United States ever accept the role of not having a role in influencing the policies of other nations? Can the United States ever view its relationship to the rest of the world without having to reduce it to a security equivalence issue?

eight

Fact or Fiction

We all tend to obsess with truth and how factual things are or should be. Our entire jurisprudence system is based on truth, the whole truth, and nothing but the truth. We like to qualify things that we say as being factual or figments of imagination (i.e., fiction). If by mistake we mix the two qualifying properties, we will be responsible for all the fuss that follows in which we will have to defend our integrity by proving lack of malice.

Yet the question is, does truth or fact exist in absolute, or is truth subject to vagaries of relativeness? Let's play a mind experiment where all the relevant facts are already presented at the outset and yet they have different perceived realities.

Let us imagine a cross junction of two roads—one going vertical (north-south) and one going horizontal (east-west). There are four people standing, one at each corner. A red van traveling south collides with a blue car traveling east, and this action is witnessed by all four individuals. For the sake of identifying individuals, let's call them A, B, C, and D, standing on the top right, top left, bottom left, and bottom right corners of the cross junction. Later, during police interviews, all of the individuals provided a summary of what happened and all agreed on the generalities of the event.

However, upon deeper questioning, they would all have some variation in their recollection of the details. Individual A would have been able to see the blue car as well as Individual D, but Individual A would have gotten to see the impact from an angle that was not available to Individual D. Therefore, Individual A might have been able to see a Bluetooth hanging from the driver's ear, which might have been distracting the driver; as a result, in Individual A's mind, the accident may have had some bearing of personal responsibility on the part of the driver in the blue car. Individual D and Individual C were perfectly positioned to see the red van driver's behavior. They both might be willing to conclude that the van was traveling too fast. But Individual C might have been able to see that the driver was distracted by kids fighting in the back seat. Individual B happened to see the accident only at the point of impact and was more in a position to see the eyes of the driver of the blue car and conclude that he was not totally present, meaning either the driver was distracted or on medication.

One event was observed by four people, and yet there is such variation in the details. This is just a simple example that doesn't take into account the hundred other variations that could be brought into play, such as the individual handicaps of the witnesses, personal prejudices, lighting variations, etc. How do you determine what is factual and what is a suggestive memory created by your mind? There is the variation to an old adage: truth is in the eyes of the beholder. How can we be sure that what we see is, in fact, what our mind supposes it is? In the field of prestidigitation (i.e., magic performance), the performers exploit the huge blind spots we have in our fields of vision and the perceptions of our visions. The sleight-of-hand tricks are all dependent on our inability to actually see even when we are looking at something. If we cannot with any guarantee rely on our visual senses to record with accuracy what we are perceiving, then what is the point of relying on visual testimony? The flaw is not just in the perceptive sensory abilities of the eyes, but rather in the translation of that information within the brain to construct an idea that makes sense. In other words, the organ that invariably is failing us is the same one we have prided ourselves on: our minds.

In Hinduism there is the concept of MAYA. Loosely put, it has been theorized to mean that the world is a divine illusion. I believe this is, at best, a gross simplification or, at worst, a total misunderstanding. I believe that one of the understandings of MAYA is the misconception that what we perceive as reality is all there is to perceive. Our perception of our reality is heavily dependent on the sensory input we receive from our five senses—sight, sound, touch, hearing, and taste. Is the reality perceived the same for people who are sensory disabled? Is it the same reality perceived for a blind as it is for a deaf person? Even among individuals who can see, the color blind have a uniquely different perception of what they see. Thus, our appreciation of our environment and our surroundings is heavily skewed by the sensitivity of our sensory organs. Even when we have perfectly functioning senses, if our brain wiring is it at fault, then again our comprehension of the same signals our senses are picking up becomes distorted. People during a migraine episode have altered perceptions and visual sensory alterations. Medications can change our psychological makeup and also our perception of reality. How can we then record or even vouch for what factual reality is if the perceiving and recording instrument is subject to so many variables and is more often than not capable of misunderstanding what it perceives?

Knowledge provides an additional capacity to understand and maybe even fuel our imagination to see what we cannot really see. Our perception of reality can be altered by imagining it differently. We now have the benefits of harnessing variant energy sources like light, electricity, gravity, and heat to enhance our living experience. In the cave-dwelling, the only source of harnessed energy came from fire. It is not that the other sources of energy did not exist back then but that we as humans had not developed our understanding and sciences and skills to either detect other sources or harness them. Is our perception of what our reality is different today than from those days? Absolutely, and in the same vein, what we know today about ourselves and our existences is limited by our capacity to imagine and the sensitivities of the instruments we have designed. The more sensitive our sensors become, the more they reveal to us our surroundings, and with that awareness comes a newer appreciation for our reality. Imagine how our concepts of reality changed once we got over the mind-set that the earth was flat and that it was the center of the universe.

But there is another possible way of looking at the concept of reality. At any given point in time, we are only aware of a facet of a viewpoint, sight, smell, or any other sensory input. It is like looking at a multifaceted prism one facet at a time. Depending on the facet you are looking through, the reality is presented to you from that viewpoint only. The belief that there is only that one viewpoint that is pertinent is also a state of illusion. In other words, try as hard as we might, we still will not be able to comprehensively understand the big picture in its entirety.

Science prides itself on its single-minded devotion to understanding nature objectively. But even within its framework, science recognizes that the models and theories it works with are only relevant until a new set of information disproves them or improves upon them. Science's factual understanding of nature is therefore not constant and is expected to constantly evolve. In science especially, it has been recognized that there are no absolute truths, only relative truth and truths that are time specific.

In short, when you are being asked to be truthful, in reality the best you can do is make an honest attempt to make a representation of your perception of the facts, which, by the way, might be completely fictional, because your mind tends to not only create convenient contextual realities, but it also vehemently protects that work creation and is therefore ultimately responsible for what is fact and fiction in your frame of reference.

nine

God!

Why do we humans need to believe in a concept like God? I know, the usual explanations are of a historical/sociological nature, such as God being the unifying force that has helped anneal together early societies, or there are the views of various theologies, by which they try to come to terms with the "miracle of life." I am also not interested in the typical debate between atheists and believers on the merits of their ideologies. I am more interested in how this concept—the need for a super being, an all-powerful entity that looks after us—has even emerged from our collective consciousness.

Across the span of time, from the disparate corners of the world, among early societies totally unconnected to one another, almost without exception some form of "God worship/fear" has always inherently emerged. There is no historical evidence that I know of that tells of a civilization, however small, that has gone about its existence without having to resort to paying obeisance to a super entity. We are the only species that resorts to this kind of behavior. Our other "intelligent" companion species do not seem to resort to anything like this. We don't see elephants, dolphins, or primates create a symbolic object for veneration. These are supposedly equally aware and intelligent species. Why is it that despite our so-called better senses and imaginative capacities, our obvious creative skills and thinking skills, and our proclivity for curiosity-driven searches that we are also absolutely susceptible to and accepting of the suggestion that there is a super being watching over us?

Is it an odd coincidence that we are the only ones on this planet who have also created an entire new species of imaginary creatures like witches, werewolves, vampires, demons, angels, superheroes, etc.? As if the real life on this planet didn't have enough challenges and dangers, we had to create imaginary sources of fear and hope from these fears.

Of all the forms of life on this planet, we are the only ones who have carved out our special status by what we have done with our collective lives. Every other species appears to function to fulfill their primary drives: seek shelter, forage for food, fight to preserve life and limb, and procreate. Beyond these, there are apparently no further attempts being made by any of these life forms to explore or enhance their senses. We humans, from the time we discovered fire, have been on an endless quest for the next big discovery. We somehow seem to be unsatisfied to exist within a status quo for too long. We dread change but simultaneously do everything to bring it about. We seem to be at our best when we are in the state of tension that accompanies transitions. This is true for changes of physical state or mental. Through our curiosity and our capacity to be enthralled by new experiences, we are ever so creatively validating our existence through the discovery and appreciation of something fantastic. In a sense, it is our personal egos and our collective knowledge of what we have accomplished through time that make us unique among all of other forms of life. Is it this apparent difference in our lives from the other fellow creatures that makes us want to believe that we are a chosen species, and if so, then by default, should it also mean that there is a chooser?

The belief in the "God" super entity is almost similar to the belief among some in astrology that attempts to link the happenings of our lives, past, present, and future, to influences from the planetary bodies and star constellations. Once again what drives us to believe that planetary bodies, which exist at such great distances from our planet, can throw about a mesh on interconnecting influences that will then affect our daily living at such a macro level? Even more importantly, that we believe we have figured out the necessary algorithms and calculations by which we can actually decipher what those influences will be is a bit presumptuous. Even with our current level of instrument sophistication, we have not been able to accurately detect the radiation being emitted from our electronic devices or their influences on our bodies with any absolute level of certainty, and these are devices within close proximity to us. How can we then be expected to qualitatively evaluate the so-called influences of these astral bodies on our minds, bodies, and fates with accuracy? Even more incredulous is that the so-called science of astrology was created centuries ago before the era of reasoning and the study of astronomy. Yet the theories of those times are still being maintained and followed today. No other discipline from those times has been maintained unchanged into the modern day.

No other, except the practices of religions.

A similar phenomenon is again expressed in a different landscape in that of stories and mythology tales. From Roman and Greek mythologies to modern-day popular comics, we have aspired to and dreamed of acquiring powers and abilities that are absolutely impossible in the real world. Humans with godlike powers and gods with human fallibilities seem to infest our creative imaginations from the earliest civilizations. Once again the questions is why. Why do we need to feel special and capable of these impossible acts? What motive does all of this serve? It does not, in any way, help us to answer the fundamental questions we often ask ourselves—who we are, what is the ultimate purpose of our existence, is there anything beyond this point of awareness, etc. Once again these stories of people with magical powers are found in all forms of civilizations from Native American folklore to early civilizations in Asia. The simple fact is that it is so universal and independent in origin that it indicates a deep inclination with in our collective minds to keep arriving at similar imaginings. The specifics might be different, but the essence is always the same.

To explore this oddity of human behavior, I am going to take a tangential approach. Imagine that you are a visitor to Earth and you are not familiar with the concept of "God" and you want someone to give you a primer on the whole concept. This would be the same as if I were to ask any person if they believed in "Wa Wa Wi Wu." Obviously, the explanation would need to be accompanied by some form of qualifying detail, definition, or description before anyone would so much as respond to this seemingly ridiculous query. Therefore, let us go about setting up a universal definition or characteristic ID for the entity called God. Without getting embroiled in religion-specific definitions, we can probably all agree that the entity called God is very simplistically defined as anything that is characteristically omnipresent, omnipotent, and omniscient. These words mean present everywhere, all powerful, and all knowing, respectively.

Now, from the perspective of an average individual, this definition by itself does not appear to be controversial. But from the perspective of the visiting alien this definition requires some more clarification. For most of us going about our daily lives, the universe is largely limited to what we see and sense around us. Therefore, in our minds, we see the reach of the God entity's powers and capacities within that perceivable universe. We fail to see the relative position we occupy in the real universe as a whole. We even fail to see the relative insignificance of our lot in the larger scheme of life on this planet itself. The perception of the alien visitor is not limited to the subjective glory of human existence alone. It would be similar to us looking at the world of ants and from the perspective of ants in an ant colony wonder why they would make such a big deal about their uniqueness and importance in their universe. To the alien the simple presence of life in its complex variations on this planet would be in itself a discovery worthy of endless amazement, not just the existence of certain life forms that communicate with vocal speech or by using writing and drawing skills to assist in communication and who also unfortunately have a God complex. So when we say that the God entity is all present, all powerful, and all knowing, the question that invariably would be posed in response would be this: Is this applicable to all of the real universe or only to a metaphorical universe of our reference only?

Let's take this logic further down its path. If we truly believe that "God" is god to the entire universe, then we have to also admit that as our awareness of what constitutes the universe changes we must be willing to concede that our "special" relationship theory with God might take a beating at the very least or more likely will be shredded to a worthless heap of words. Alternatively, we might have to place limits on what we determine as the universe of relevance in order to keep our definition of the concept of God valid. Mind you, the idea of a super entity called God is not being questioned here. The focus is on the ludicrous logic we as humans have created around this concept to accommodate it in our lives despite the evidence to the contrary. This special relationship that we have mythologized is mostly to confer and confirm a special place for our existence in nature, which is why even the identity of God has humanlike characteristics.

To bring perspective back, let's ask a basic question: If God were like us or we were created in his image (a convoluted way of saying that God was humanlike), then it would mean that we have a special place in the ecosystem of this planet and possibly of the universe. If we managed to hypothetically destroy all of the existent life on the planet, what are the prospects of our survival even with the advantages we have with our technologies? I would guess pretty much zero. If the reverse was true and the entire human race disappeared, what would that do to life on the planet? I have one word for that: *flourish*. In other words, we need the other life forms on the planet to survive; the other life forms are not dependent on our existence to survive. Admittedly, in the example above I cheated a bit for the effect of dramatic comparison. The actual equivalent scenario of our extinction would not be that of the extinction of all nonhuman life forms but of a selective few, but even with that, the changes in the ecosystems would be enough to destroy our standards of living. But more to the point, we are the only ones capable of wiping out life around us if we chose to do so. No other naturally rival organism has the desire or lifestyle engineered to singularly extinguish the human race. Even the lowly bacterial and viral infection vectors have a self-limiting capacity to inflict damage. Humans, on the other hand, without even consciously trying to, have managed to wipe out several species. If humans were made in God's form, wouldn't it have made more sense that God's "special creation" be more deferential in the use of natural resources and be naturally inclined to guard and protect and nurture those resources rather than almost cannibalistically eating up and polluting the very environment it has to lie in?

Thus, to the visiting alien the fundamental flaw of the God concept will be that the definition we have created does not reconcile with the practices we have authorized in the name of the entity. All forms of God worship run on a simple thought: Be good or be punished. Be obediently deferential to the super entity, but also be accepting of the wrath and anger of God for perceived misbehavior. Doesn't this behavior resemble some other form of familiar societal order? How about life under feudal rule? Under kings, queens, and regents, we have historically, as a collective, been subjected to abuse of power and demands to observe ridiculous obedience practices. Is it then a coincidence that we have copied such an abusive relationship into our model of our relationship with God? In some religions, we even accord God the title and form of a king, with all the trappings of a royal court.

If God is truly omnipresent, omnipotent, and omniscient, why does God need us to declare our undying love and obedience to it, and why do we believe that by leading a special type of lifestyle deferential to the supposed edicts of God that our prayers will receive differential treatment? Is this not the logic of prayer before embarking on a venture? Why is there a prayer session by an individual or a team before a sporting event? For an entity so vastly encumbered by the goings-on in the universe, what possible motive does it have to selectively side with any one side or individual?

Astrology

Let us leave the God paradox for yet another paradox: our indulgence in practices that supposedly help in predictions. Astrology is one of them. From the early days of human existence, we have always had a fascination for things we saw up in the sky, especially at night. Even today lying under a cloudless sky in an area of pristine air quality invokes feelings of awe and a sense of wonder at the miracle of cosmic vastness and the beauty of the multitude of twinkling points of light. In ancient times, in addition to wonder, I am certain people's feelings were also mixed with some concern and trepidation. Shooting stars, the cyclic appearance of moon phases, eclipses, and star location, etc., might have been taxing on our evolving imaginations. As soon as a pattern was recognized in the regular appearances of these stellar shows, inevitably some tried to correlate it to the events, good or bad, of their lives. If the arrival of a complete solar eclipse accompanied an epidemic, then it became a bad omen. We humans have an infinite capacity of association, especially when it comes to the negative. We remember with great clarity how a particular bad event happened in association with another event and draw from that the eternal caution of avoiding the combination of the two activities.

As we have gone down this road of precarious logic, we have built up the belief that these astral bodies have a way of influencing our lives and that we can calculate that influence and make predictions about the effects of that influence. In the early societies, the role of dabbling in scientific inquiry, appeasing the gods, evolving medical remedies, and predicting the weather, at least as a tool for farming or hunting, fell on the shoulders of one man or a group of individuals. Among the neo-paleontological cultures like the ancient Native Americans, this individual would be the iconic medicine man/woman. In other societies, this group of individuals might have been the priests of a temple. As our knowledge base expanded, the duties of medicine man/woman, God worship, weatherman, soothsayer, etc., became assigned to separate individuals. But since they all believed in the same basic logic, there was a lot of overflow of influences from one discipline to the other. For example, early medical practices had a prayer requirement for success, and in some instances the remedies had to be administered at certain times of the day for maximum potency. I do not find a flaw in this thought logic, as a lot of the prescriptions were drawn from a compilation of observable associations between a set of actions and their effects.

Of all the disciplines that evolved, the disciplines that related to the physical sciences and medical sciences had an advantage over the disciplines of religion and soothsaying, and star reading. The former disciplines had subject matter at hand to test their theories for validity. Their theories could be verified or disproved and in doing so would help modify the understanding of a process. Religion, astrology, and soothsaying were heavy on theory but had no way of coming up with a method to verify theories. In other words, they depended on faith for their existence and relevance. They had to construct a logic that was acceptable to the masses.

How can one convince entire populations to believe in something that cannot be proven? How can one come up with a belief system that can be accepted by subsequent generations and with minimal effort? How can an intelligent, self-aware, creative, imaginative species be gullible enough to blindly follow such a thought construct without proof?

For all the strengths we possess as a species and all the achievements we have accomplished through the centuries, we all have a common deep-rooted flaw within our psyche. We are all constantly living in a state of fear—fear of the unknown, fear of the unseen, fear of the potential of uncertainties that the future brings, and now even fear of danger from situations and creations delivered from our wild imaginations. Since we can imagine, we can anticipate all forms of dangers and harms that we are always trying to find a way out of if not by beating the odds at least predicting the odds so that we might be better prepared. This is where the art of soothsaying becomes important. Ignorance is best countered, in the absence of real knowledge, with a lot of confident bluster. The need for bluster is important to people who dabble in future predictions, as they cannot rely on evidence to convince anyone of the predictions' validity.

Matching our fear of the unknown is our need for easily acceptable explanations for events that go wrong in our lives. Combining the ability of future predictions with the explanation of the chaotic nature of life events into a neat little story line is what astrology, palm reading, and psychic and tarot reading is meant to accomplish.

Consider the source to understand the flaws within the information being dispersed. Astrological protocols and charts were developed in the centuries before Christ (BC). Telescopes came into existence in the seventeenth century AD and have since been progressively been improved upon. The information we have today, gathered with the help of a variety of telescopes and other tools, about the composition of our astral companions is phenomenally greater than the information that was used to create the astrological protocols. Astrology did not incorporate these new findings as and when they happened and evolve their protocols to keep up with the expanding awareness. To put things into perspective, if the star constellation information is considered as a map, then astrologists have used that information to derive an inference that serves their proclivity to prognosticate, while the astronomers have used the same map for more practical uses like navigational tools, tide patterns observation, etc. Furthermore, the map being referenced by the astrologers is an ancient one. If we were to do size comparison based on the information difference between the knowledge used to construct the astrological parameters and today's astronomical awareness, then it would be like comparing a piece of scrap paper (astrological map) to a huge canvas of information (astronomical map).

By any standards of expectation, one would expect the lesser-information source to be less accurate and less relevant than the larger information source. Yet we choose to dabble in attempting to predict the happenings of our lives using an ancient system that bases its theories on knowledge that is extremely outdated and has been disproven multiple times. The individual need to believe in the efficacy of this pseudoscience cannot be better illustrated than in what happened in one of the most populous nations recently. **A high court in India in 2011 passed a judgment declaring astrology as a valid science and worthy of being taught in a university!**

Mythology of Supermen

Throughout our vastly varied history, we have conjured up stories of fantastic and often magical people. We have used them as vehicles to emphasize valuable moral, legal, and cultural points to our fellow citizens. Societal rules and individual mores can be instructed to anyone but with no guarantee of either being remembered or followed effectively by the population at large. However, if these same rules and mores are presented within a framework of a story, then, with the stories, the validity and essence of the instruction carries on in people's imaginations, with minimal need for monitoring and micromanaging—an impossible task for a single individual let alone an entire population. With the creation and adoption of these tales, societal life gets modified and in time becomes responsible for giving each regional population their unique cultural identity and flavor.

This ancient habit of relying on unrealistically created super beings to guide us, cajole us, and admonish us to lead "moral" lives has continued to this day. Now we express the same desire for the stories of the fantastic through our modern version of "gods"—superheroes. Besides, they make absolutely wonderful story-telling vehicles through which one can let one's imagination run wild. With each of these creations, we have also restructured the logic, at least temporarily, that pertains to how life runs. Things that we do not encounter in real life we can bring into creation through print or through audio-visual mediums. We can compensate for what we deem as our shortcomings through these stories. Our worst fears throughout our historical existence now have a place where they can be enhanced or easily neutralized, and all for an entertainment reason without having to suffer any really bad side effects. Thus, through these stories we have created alternate possibilities of lives and beings who can compensate for our mortality and our susceptibility to old age, disease, and injustices, as well as fulfill our wild desires to be able to fly, have incredible strengths, travel through space and time, visit different planets, and meet aliens, those that are horrifying or evolved.

Entertaining as these stories might be, they are also the reflection of some of the deep-seated issues within our psyche, the same ones that have led us through time to create the "God" movement and the fortune-telling crafts. These are the same primordial fears of the unknown, the unseen, and the unexplainable and also the hopes and aspirations for something better. Through these stories we attempt to compensate and prevail upon our deep-seated mental demons.

"What If" and Other Explanations

So what has made an intelligent, creative, and imaginative species get tangled up in irrational and illogical thought constructs that have then become so deeply integrated into the collective consciousness of all societies?

I believe there are two opposing driving forces for this eventuality. The first is our ingrained persistent curiosity. From the earliest of our days, we have all been asking ourselves almost constantly one critical question: What if? This is more than a curiosity question; it is a curiosity question that precedes an action. It is different from the what, where, why, or when questions. Those are, I deem, inertia questions, in that the answers they seek might only be to academically answer a query without really affecting the status or course of action. The "What if" question, on the other hand, pertains to impending action planning, and it usually precedes a change in course of action that is being considered. Our curiosity has fueled our persistent exploratory behavior, but on the road of discovery we have encountered frequently formidable obstacles and hazards. If we were lesser in spirit, our enterprising quests would have ended there. (I mean the quests to be both physical as well as mental.) However, at every one of these crucial junctures we have asked the "What if" question to break the mental logjam and chart an alternate route around the obstacle. Obstacle surmounting is hardwired in our minds. Every time we encounter an apparently impossible obstacle we eventually figure out a way to get past it, and that solution is invariably the result of many "What if" questions that our mind conjures up. No other species or life form we know of indulges in this format of decision making. To me, this one question, through millennium, has been singularly responsible for all the technological breakthroughs we have made and are continuing to make. Of course, I might be overstating it a bit.

The second force, like the second half of the yin-yang symbol, does the exact opposite of what our innate curiosity would have us do. It is the one that cautions our approach. It is the one that constantly keeps us on our toes by instilling the fear of the unknown, the unseen, and the unexplained. It acts as the deadweight or ballast to our roaring, reckless exploration. If uncontained, this inherent fear would grow to dominance and incapacitate any progress. The reason we have created the Gods and prophecy making is probably to counter this second force.

Fear is an emotional response, albeit an irrational one. One cannot rationalize one's way out of fear. Fear needs to be confronted with an overwhelming boost of confidence and courage. In the absence of facts, which is usually the domain in which fear emerges, hope and promise of prevailing over any danger can only be stimulated by using powerful story tools to provide examples for emotional courage. Using the God phenomenon, not only can courage be instilled, but one is also admonished to deliberately put oneself in harm's way to accomplish a greater good, all in the name of the God, and to be blessed for the effort. To be able to do this, a paradigm of trust and faith in the super entity has to be created wherein all that we are unaware of, which is bound to be the source of our fear, happens to be known by this super entity. Therefore, even if we are sailing blind the super entity would guide us past the obstacles. With that kind of belief, we can answer the "What if" questions with less trepidation and hesitancy.

Even if we choose not to be ambitiously exploratory and are content with living a mundane existence, we will not be free of risks and dangers. Life on this planet is one of being constantly in a state of preparation to counter or compensate for dangers. Our bodies are constantly under the threat of attack from things, some of which we cannot even see, like bacteria and viruses to larger organisms. Our lives are challenged by natural disasters like earthquakes, floods, fires, and extreme weather conditions. There is no predictability in our relationships with one another. Our human relationships are fraught with ambiguity and trust issues.

We cannot even trust ourselves individually to be consistent and predictable. Mental disease, mood variations, and genetic disabilities all make us capable of increased self-risk. Therefore, even within our mundane existences, we at times can feel under siege.

Our animal cousins are just as aware of the physical dangers this planet poses for them. They react to events like fires, earthquakes, and floods much like we do, but within their collective they do not possess the memory of the results of living in the danger zones of the planet. They might be aware of the dangers on an instinctive level, but unlike us they are not forewarned by the experiences of others. We have, through our linguistic and story-telling skills, created a collective memory of the dangers we have to live with. If we choose to continue to live in these areas despite what we know, it is more a testament to our exploratory and risk-tempting nature.

This level of awareness of unpredictability can be overwhelming. It would give us immense comfort if we could somehow have a way of predicting the dangers and then set about compensating for them. This is where the need for prophecy arises. Not only does prophecy, within its own logic, supposedly predict, but it also prescribes the solutions for the predicaments we would face. In most instances, believers happily entwine this rationale with that of the innate theological belief system. If the details of our daily lives can be believed to be ordained by a super entity or super entities, then it makes perfect sense to placate them in order to find a relief from our misfortunes.

Even the more sober members of the population who are pragmatic and do not feel the need to dabble in superstition to manage their affairs cannot help wonder occasionally "What if" there was some truth in the field of prophecy. Our innate curiosity actually will, at times, help fuel the belief in the improbable. Besides, who does not like to dabble in fantasy every once in a while? The thrill or satisfaction or comfort it can promise can be very seductive. No human is aware of all that is to be known; therefore, how can one very emphatically reject the logic of prophecy and the God belief? It is difficult to disprove a negative, especially when the object of negation has been summoned into existence by our own innate insecurities and fears.

Faith and Belief

Admittedly, the dangers of living on this planet notwithstanding, we are also subjected to stresses and trauma from within our own minds. While there may not be much we can do in terms of the natural dangers we face, we can implement strategies to help us in regard to our own psychiatric creations. The beliefs in the super entity and the projected effects of our planetary neighbors help in our ability to contain the vagaries of our "fates" to manageable stress levels. In medicine, there is the concept of panacea, which in essence is using an inactive agent to produce the same effect as an active agent devoid of any side effects. Our belief systems help establish the equivalent of panacea moments in our dealings with our life stresses. To that end, I have no objections to one's choosing to dabble in the "God" systems. The problem surfaces when the same belief system interferes with accurate logical decision making or when it supplants self-reliance with dependence and worse renders someone susceptible to being manipulated.

We perform better when we are charged with a purpose. It may be a self-motivated goal or an external admonishment to rise above one's diffidence and perform at a higher level of competence. The pep talk one gets before a game or the rallying cry to arms before a political event are both examples of external motivations to make people break out of their shells and participate and perform. A multibillion-dollar industry thrives on dealing with self-motivation issues. Religion and prophecy making are the original self-motivation enterprises from the earliest times. For the believer, the downturns in their fate, which they would have encountered multiple times in their lives, are usually not capable of rendering them hopeless. Believers take great comfort and solace in their beliefs and use them to weather the tough times. Devoid of faith, many individuals would rather have given up on this whole living enterprise and checked themselves out. It is a testament to the faith and belief of the various populations that they have survived wars, natural disasters, and personal losses through the ages and still continue to live on and bring into existence subsequent generations in hope of better times. These generations do well to learn from their elders about faith and belief. God belief is therefore central to the survival and the continued evolution of the human race down from the ancient times to now.

Some of the laudable achievements of humans are attributed to their having faith and doing good and being moral. Our almost delusional belief in measuring up to the standards of a higher moral authority has guided political movements, like nonviolence and abolitionist movements against slavery, and also the various social organizations that have come into existence to aid the poor and the destitute, like the Red Cross and Mother Teresa's Missionaries of Charity, and yet......the story of humans is also littered with instances of abuses, wars, and genocides in the name of a God. If religious beliefs can be manipulated to cause, such subjugation and harm, why were they not abolished by rulers in the interest of their populations? Didn't religious beliefs in some way threaten rulers' control of the masses?

It was because they, more than anybody else, recognized that through the aegis of religious edicts the population could be made more manageable. Imagine traditional society existing within a framework of laws only. The laws are only effective if they are followed by the citizens. But how does one ensure such deliberate obedience? If the rulers of the state are of a highly suspicious disposition, then they will flood the society with individuals tasked with spying on fellow citizens looking for infractions and instituting a very aggressive punishment regimen. Dictatorships function in this modality. (Dictatorships are also usually atheistic, as religious people are more resilient and less likely to be subjugated). But these are people- and time-intensive endeavors. Furthermore, in this type of society, there are never enough individuals to complete the task of absolute surveillance. Therefore, the better approach is to pass laws and have people be personally charged with maintaining good faith and self-policing themselves. If they buy into the God concept, then it becomes easy to direct them to do right by God or else face the possibility of divine repercussions. Thus religion has been a very effective tool in managing developing societies.

It has also been used to justify regal indiscretions. Just as rulers used religion to help control their masses, the religious theocratic order also used rulers to enhance their influence and hold. They could stifle valid questions being asked to understand the intricacies of life. Science and health decisions had to be approved by the religious bodies or science and health proponents ran the risk of being accused of heresy, or worse, of being in collusion with the "devil." The religious bodies had to maintain this kind of control or with new discoveries their legitimacy would be called into question. Through heavy-handed methods, they injected their influence in every aspect of daily life.

When Galileo first published his astronomy findings and made the declaration that the sun, rather than the earth, is the center of the system of planetary bodies (our solar system), he was hauled before the Inquisition Court and threatened with consequences of being convicted of heresy. He was forced to submit a written redaction of his findings. No thought process was permitted unless it had been previously sanctioned by the religious order of the society. Rules of daily living, societal interactions, family interrelationship protocols concerning matters of trade and tradecraft, entertainment, etc., were and are subject to direct or indirect influence by the religious order. This influence is further reinforced through regular, routine conditioning of the mind through prayer services at places of worship. These prayer services eventually attain a level of familiarity, and society looks upon them as a harmless chore they partake in time and again. (*The more benevolent schools of religious thought would have emphasized the aspects of tolerance and acceptance and a more abstract sense of philosophies of life. The more rigid religious schools of thought would have dogmatically followed a rigid interpretation of the religious rules and would have emphasized the concept of punishment, showing inflexibility in dealing with infractions of religious doctrines and believing in personal suffering as penance, and they would demand frequent proof of belief by some form of sacrifice.*)

Ultimately, irrespective of the logic for the existence of a super entity, its persistence in the human imagination would not have survived so many centuries if not for the continuous maintenance and propagation of the idea by the few who have had vested interest in its perpetuation. The resonance faith has on individual lives leads these individuals to their higher calling, which is usually an exercise in virtue. The horrors and misdemeanors executed in the name of a God are usually the result of human ego, avarice, power hunger, and criminal psychosis. Ultimately, on balance, the final judgment on the logic of belief in God and other superstitions rests on each person's individual experience. For those who are inclined to be susceptible to the fear of the unknown, such belief will offer comfort and will be further reinforced in the absence of any negative exposure through the practice of believing. The ones who have suffered at the hands of the religious orthodoxy or the fickle turns of fate will question its relevance even at the risk of being excommunicated from their social circles.

Even among individuals who proclaim that they are nonbelievers in respect to God and prophecy crafts, many subscribe to some form of personal belief system. We cannot exist without a belief in something. They might believe in themselves. Belief is what gets us going about our routines every day. In the absence of religious beliefs, we substitute them with nonreligious beliefs. Belief in science can also be taken to its extremes where it can start to dabble in the illogical. Accidents that happen in pursuit of scientific glory are usually the result of someone being deluded by the belief that scientifically one is informed enough that he or she can plan around any problem. In some circles even science begins to taken on an absolutist avatar and begins to resemble the religious orders. In these circles, individuals establish a similar hierarchy of control of dissemination and utilization of scientific thought, become dogmatic in their observances of protocols, and institute just as rigorous a punishment regimen for those who defy the rule makers. One example that leaps to mind is the close-minded approach that Western medical schools have in regard to Eastern formats of treating the human body. Until recently, the practices of acupuncture and yogic meditation were dismissed with scant regard. The flaw in all these systems of human endeavor, religious or nonreligious, is more often the result of our own failings and insecurities by which we corrupt whatever enterprise we apply ourselves to.

ten

Identity and Death

When we compare the two states of life and death, we are actually comparing the two states of an individual, one with a projected identity and one where this identity is completely absent. Life that we respond to is, in essence, an affirmation of our identity. An organism's mechanics of living are not interesting beyond the point of scientific curiosity until identity is included. In death, it is not the end of the living process that is bereaved as much as the termination of the projection of the identity. As living, breathing organisms, we are all alike in most respects. The individual variations that we see expressed through our likes and dislikes and our unique idiosyncrasies make us uniquely individual. This is true not just for humans but also for a lot of other animals. Life exists from single-cell organisms onward to more complex beings like us, yet the act of dying is uniquely palpable in species that have an aura of individualism, or what we colloquially call personality. Plants and trees both die, but then why does their death not cause the same sense of loss we feel when we lose a pet animal or a fellow human?

Imagine a human being who is lying on a hospital bed. If this individual were to lose his or her limbs, would that change the way one would view that individual? Will that person be considered a lesser individual for having fewer body parts? What if we took it to the extreme and imagined the individual to basically be a head attached to hospital equipment, alive and emoting, but only a head. Would this extreme shape make the person a lesser person? Yes, to some extent. For all expectations of what a person is, someone who can physically do things in addition to possessing mental capabilities, this body-less individual would be considered extremely handicapped, but still a person nevertheless. What if it the individual's body is physically intact but the person is incapable of emoting or communicating, such as someone who has sustained severe head trauma, possibly with missing brain tissue? Though, for all appearances, the person looks whole, yet functionally, he or she is no more alive than a laboratory specimen. Would such a person evoke the same human interaction sensibilities? Probably not. In other words, the people we acknowledge as people are essentially the ones with fully functional heads.

Let us then focus on the head. What aspect of the head is the one that we respond to? Is it the facial anatomy (i.e., the parts like ear, nose, mouth, eyes, etc.) or is it the functioning of the mind behind the anatomical features? If the mind could communicate using a laptop, would we treat the head with the same respect that we would treat it when it is fully functional?

We are taken up by the robot-animatronics field, which attempts to replicate every detail of the human head, including the individual muscle movements. But in the end we know we are dealing with a machine, because despite the increased sophistication with which robots resemble real people, they cannot articulate an original thought. Devoid of thought, we know they are machines. Therefore, identity is tied more to the ability of an individual to enunciate thinking. Personality is a manifestation of an individual's ego and from it flows the method by which it interacts with the world around it. Intellect and personality make up a person's identity. Death is the end of this identity.

Self-Identity

The individual human story is one of either creating an identity or assimilating into a created identity. We all stress ourselves out in trying to become someone, and we showcase our success in measures of wealth, possessions, power, importance, and finally titles. We all know that this entire finely choreographed existential dance will come to an end some-day. We also are aware that we know nothing about what happens to us or our identities when we die. We are also just as aware that everything we acquire in this lifetime has no value at the point of our transition into death. All the glory or infamy with which we surround our lives gets neu-tralized to nothingness at death. Assigning potentially endless value for what we do in this life with ramifications beyond death is the reason why we have the religious concept of post-life reward or punishment being meted out to our good deeds or sins. If our existence results in nothing that can be transferred across to the realms of the dead, then why do we spend entire lifetimes and more trying to outdo one another? Animal instincts with regard to shelter, food, mate, and procreation aside, why do we even bother with development and evolving aspirations?

Our lives have a definite beginning as well as a definite but unpredict-able ending. The time we have in between needs to be spent in a manner that will not cause us to become moribund. It is not enough to exist as other creatures and fellow animals. We would be bored to death if we existed only to eat, mate, and move around with no defined purpose until our deaths. The curse of intellectualism forces us to exist beyond the physical plane. We need to exist with meaning at an abstract level too. The possessions we acquire, the competitions we participate in with ourselves or others, and the pride we take in our capacity to achieve goals and targets are all motivational tools that assist us in our living journey help us to find meaning where none may have existed otherwise. Even the individuals who have forsaken the race to acquisitions are charged with purpose to find other channels of self-fulfillment. The monks who exist in solitude and in silence are indulged in a battle within their minds to conquer the unconquerable instincts of humans, and in attempting to do so they will eventually achieve a personal goal.

Time can be an ally as much as a brutal foe. Those who are not inclined to participate in life because of an innate sense of the ulti-mate futility of all human endeavors or because of mental incapacities end up prematurely terminating their lives. These are the individuals in whom the sense of self-identity has been compromised or lost. Purpose informs one's identity, and a sense of identity fuels the journey of life in quest of a purposeful goal. The identity less existence is filled with unending pain: physical, emotional, and psychological. This pain can be chronic debilitating or acute and deep-cutting. Most individuals will in their lifetime experience momentary lapses of purpose. Most of them will learn to soldier on, and they will learn that what drives them through the mental morass is their belief in finding something better. Sense of purpose provides the road map for the long walk through life, and belief is what spurs the motivation to continue on the path. Suicidal individuals lack a sense of purpose and do not believe that they will find one.

Sense of identity stemming from a personal goal or purpose is different for each individual. Some may have their identity tied to their physicality, their physical prowess, or their sense of physical completeness. When some of these individuals become permanently maimed or handicapped physically, then they cannot tolerate the loss of wholeness, and with that their sense of self becomes altered. Some of these individuals will end up attempting suicide. Alternatively, others may be proud of what they can achieve through their other faculties like sight, voice, and mind. When these faculties get compromised, the individuals more likely to attempt ending their lives would be the ones unable to compensate and find alternate modes of expression. Their inner sense of being has lost its purpose. Debilitating incapacitation or pain can drain the desire or the energy required to keep up the effort to live on. Depression is usually due to an individual's inability to find empowerment through his or her pursuit of goals or to believe in his or her visions of purpose. Every individual will face these temporary disconnects with his or her inner core, but the resilient will eventually prevail through sheer desire to live or just stubbornness in not giving in to one's inner demons. We put so much effort in creating a mythology about our lives just to live them out.

Death

What happens at the point of death is a subject of many academic and not-so-academic viewpoints. What happens to the organism physiologically and functionally has been revealed through research. But my pointed focus is on what happens to the individual and when. Obviously I do not possess any special inkling on the death process that allows me to lay out the answers to these eternal questions. However, there is no harm in following the process as logic would permit and deriving from it some interesting observations.

At the transition between living and dead, there must be a critical moment when the living consciousness ceases. Is there a dead consciousness that then takes over? In our living state, even though we are who we are through the functioning of our minds, we see ourselves in our complete physical state in possession of all our anatomical parts and faculties. Quadriplegics are known to dream of themselves in their whole, undamaged state. Therefore, our physical form provides us with a matrix in our minds where we can seat our consciousness. In death, the physical form is lost. Where would a consciousness reside? Will it seek a physical construct to align with, or are the rules of logic different when dead? One more fundamental question: Why should we assume there is a consciousness past the point of death? What purpose would that serve? If it did exist, would it be as individualistic as the living consciousness, or would it be a vague, ephemeral consciousness, a part of some kind of pan-universe consciousness?

The answers we seek are in many respects clouded by preconceptions and misconceptions we have about death and the process of dying. Our cultures and belief systems have trained us overtly or covertly think in some definite thought patterns only.

To understand death will bring greater sense of perspective to the task of living. When one dies, according to the various schools of thought, which are usually influenced heavily by the religious disposition of the culture, either one goes into an alternate existence mode while retaining all of the memories, hopes, dreams, and affiliations to their fellow human cotravelers, or they might be reassigned to another new life—reincarnation. Before we start to dabble with these concepts, we have to first grapple with the whole concept of a soul.

What is a soul? Is it a person's essence? If so, what are its origins? Is it organic in its origin, created with life? Or is it a part of the ephemeral universal awareness, temporarily cleaved to join with the developing consciousness of a life form? Are we confusing our wakefulness, our consciousness, for our soul? Is there an equivalent form of soul to all forms of life? Do even the single-cell organisms have a soul, or is having a soul only a component of intelligent types of lives? The human population has been growing constantly. There was a time when the global population was only one billion people, and now it is over six billion. Does that mean that the soul populations are also increasing, and if so, is there a maximum number of souls that can exist? Do souls have individual traits? Do they have memory of the organic lives lived? Do they relate to other souls the way we relate to other humans? These questions do not lead to any definite answers. The answers one arrives at are the ones that are most comfortable to live with.

If the soul is merely our sense of being and awareness, then at death it ceases too, in which case all scenarios of an afterlife are irrelevant. If soul, on the other hand, is that intangible entity, the abstract component that gives meaning to living organisms, then does it have an existence devoid of the corporeal form it becomes associated with? To play the devil's advocate, let me hypothesize that much like energy has many ways of manifesting itself (i.e., light, heat, magnetism etc.), what if awareness was also a manifestation of universal energy? It could then exist independent of an organic vessel, but it might be devoid of any specificity. Once it is bonded to a life form, it then takes on a localized relevance. Then, when it departs the life form, does it return to its native form of nonspecific awareness, or does it contain a resonance of the life it was invested with? If this were true, then there would be the possibility of endless souls being created from universal energy.

What if there is no soul to live on after death? Does that change the way we would behave? Is the idea of souls an extension of our desire for immortality? Or is it our desire to retain our kith and kinship relationships by which we define our cultural and genetic roots? Of course our egos also require some validation. If death negates everything we associate with life, then in a way it negates our own existence. But what if the miracle of life is much more than our petty egos and desires? What if the life we have on this planet is the only form of living that exists in the entire universe? We all hypothesize the probability of life in other planetary systems. Logically, that is to be expected. But we have not yet encountered life elsewhere with any certainty. In fact, our scientists would be delighted with the discovery of any form of life in other planetary objects, even single-cell organisms. We have set the bar for discovery this low because of the near-impossible odds of coming in contact with an advanced form of life.

Even if life exists in other planetary systems, they might be just as limited in their abilities to travel through space. If a tree falls in a forest and nobody is there to witness it, did it really fall? If life exists in other places in the universe but are just incapable of revealing these other life forms, then do they really exist? We have to contend with the here and now because these are the tangible elements of our environment. If you look at the life that we surround ourselves with, in all its diversity and tones, and then realize that perhaps this unique mistake of molecular interaction is nowhere else present and is on its own nonreplicable, then you begin to get a sense of the sheer immenseness of the importance of our existence. That in itself is much more miraculous than all the miracle creations spun from our imaginations. That sense of being in the midst of and being a part of the ongoing creation of life (*I mean* creation *in its most secular sense*) against astronomical odds is the closest the spiritually inclined will get to being witnesses to the imagined spectacle and intent of God.

If that were true, then the life we lead is a one-time deal. It is akin to being granted entry to a phenomenal cosmic theme park-style roller coaster of an experience. If the ride gets too hectic, we have in our powers the ability to choose to exit the ride, but with the realization that it's an irrevocable decision. Alternatively, if we can hang in there and refuse to give in, we might be in for an incredible journey, which will, of course, end at the exit door. We might not remember any of it after we have exited, or worse we might not even be aware anymore. But for the relatively short duration that we are immersed in the experience, it will be a unique one. It does not promise to be benign in its effects. Along with great joys and triumphs, we will experience the sorrows, pain, uncertainties, and various afflictions of the mind and body and spirit. But it is an experience unlike any other form of existence. Even at the worst of times, drenched in discomfort and suffering, remember that all that is being experienced will end at the time we exit the arena, with no further reverberations or effects. For a piece of inconsequential stardust floating though time and space, this is the rarest of rare opportunities to feel alive even for a short spell. *That* is the gift of life. Death is the return to status quo before we are granted the grand lottery of life.

eleven

Bags of Chemical Gel Soup!

Obesity is an epidemic in the United States. This declaration has been valid for at least the two decades that I have been here. The United States is also a country of immigrants. It has been populating its citizenry ranks with foreigners for as long as it has been an independent country, and some years before that too. But for the native indigent population, the vast majority of Americans have a genetic lineage that begins in other parts of the globe. Obesity is not an epidemic in most of those countries, at least historically speaking. What, then, has happened to the genetic material on its crossing over the Pacific or Atlantic Oceans to result in such a dramatic alteration that the populations arising thereafter from the same genetic mix have become victims to an epidemic of obesity? Obesity, however, appears to be largely the affliction of the resident population more than the immigrant population. Therefore, it seems to have skipped the generation of individuals who crossed over the oceanic divides and struck their offspring instead. Why and how?

The erstwhile underdeveloped countries have recently entered a phase of rapid development and relative prosperity. Here, too, one of the hallmarks of their newfound prosperity is the rise in obesity among their ranks. Most of these nations do not have a large immigrant population to compare themselves against. Here again the obesity epidemic appears to favor the younger and newer generations.

Alcoholics and drug addicts have a different kind of alteration of their physiology. Long-term alcoholics and drug addicts undergo permanent change in the way their bodies function, so much so that even if they were to sober up they would not be able to revert back to their old way of functioning. But in this class of individuals, too, the effect of chemical alcohol or recreational drugs is variable. Some are more prone than others to succumb to addiction. Why?

Our bodies, their organic functions and even our minds, thoughts, sense of self, awareness, consciousness, and intellect, are all manifestations of the multitude of chemical interactions that take place daily. We are one walking, breathing chemical factory with thousands of chemicals at play with one another. Each of us has a body that began with a certain chemical makeup. Unlike other markers of our identity, namely fingerprints, or DNA, the chemical makeup of our bodies is subject to change, some periodic, some occasional, induced by external and internal triggers. The periodic changes are the changes we encounter every day through a daily cycle. The body produces more steroids in the morning hours, which is why surgeons schedule surgeries in the wee hours of the morning to maximize on the benefits of naturally produced steroids. Our bodies burn calories faster in the first third of the day—again, a reason for the advice to have a hearty breakfast. Other periodic chemical changes are like the ones women go through with their monthly cycles. The occasional changes are the ones related to the aging of the body.

From the baby stage to old age, we go through continuous, but gradual, changes to our chemical composition. These changes are not smooth, but occur in fits and starts. The classic example is the bodily changes that become apparent in the teenage years. Other changes occur when people reach middle age and old age. The chemical changes that can be directly associated with extrinsic factors are the responses people have to the intake of chemical substances like alcohol or drugs. An example of an intrinsic change to body chemistry is someone experiencing a stress attack that leads to changes in blood pressure. The effects of the types of lives we lead on our body chemistry are responsible for a whole host of our current existential issues, from body weight issues to mental health issues. Since we do not have much say in the gene pool we come from, we can be excused for wanting some aspects of our health, body type, life span, etc., to be different. However, in addition to the challenges of our genetics, we complicate our prospects of leading contended, healthy lives by the choices we make in what we imbibe or eat.

In India, where poverty and politics have made ensuring healthy and adequate nutrition a multigenerational challenge, there is a certain desire for people to fatten up babies. I am not sure if this has anything to do with projecting an image of relative prosperity or a belief that the fatter the babies become, the more likely they will be to survive the gauntlet of infections and diseases or occasional periods of starvation that await them. One of the ways by which they fatten babies is by feeding them rolled-up balls of butter. The taste and smell of butter or clarified butter, called ghee, remains with the person for life. In fact, in later life, the way to showcase good cooking is to always lace food with ghee for the smell.

Obesity

Introducing a developing child's body to this type of fatty challenge sets about changes in the way the child deals with excess calories for the rest of his or her life. Excess calories are usually stored as fat in cells specifically designed for fat storage. Much like every other cell in the body, the total number of cells of any given tissue in the body is determined partly by genetics and partly by the work the tissues have to contend with, especially during the developmental stages. This is why kids who participate in sports from early childhood develop athletic form and physique. The latecomers to an active lifestyle will be able to bulk up their muscles and achieve the appearance of athletic form, but they will not be able to perform with the same ease with which the early entrants into the sporting disciplines perform. Muscle cells and fat cells respond almost identically when subject to loading. In the developing years, they compensate by producing as many cells as possible in addition to enlarging existing cells (increasing storage capacity while at the same time increasing utilization of current storage). In late bloomers this balance is skewed more in favor of enlarging existing cells, as the window for rapid cell multiplication has closed. Therefore, an early fatty load leads to more fatty cells.

People who come into a high-calorie diet later in life will also become obese, but the obesity will be through enlarging the limited fat deposit cells. Of the two, the latter will therefore find it easier to lose weight than those exposed to fats early in their lives. The simple addition of fats in the diet during the childhood years determines the propensity for those individuals to have weight gain issues for the rest of their lives. This tweaking of body chemistry in the early childhood days sets into motion permanent structural changes and a host of future challenges: body image issues, self-confidence issues, and genuine health issues connected with obesity, such as diabetes, blood pressure problems, and eventually cardiac conditions. For many this early exposure to fats will also dictate the lifestyle choices these individuals will make. Most will seek sedentary lifestyles and might be prone to mood disorders.

The same effect is noticed in children of developed nations too. The chemicals they ingest in the form of refined sugars, fats, and preservatives all play a role in changing their body chemistry irrevocably. Some of the food preservatives, coloring agents, and antibiotics, in combination with the fats and sugars, will change the hormonal chemistry, and these children will become trapped in a ceaseless battle to achieve a relatively stable lifestyle and healthy existence. Children who become obese early on face an uphill battle to stay healthy throughout their lives. People who once lived an active lifestyle who become fat in later life still possess most of the muscle mass they developed during the growing-up stages and therefore can get back to a healthier body status fairly easily. Obesity in childhood is accompanied by a sedentary lifestyle, which prevents the buildup of muscles. These individuals find it more difficult to lose weight because of inadequate muscle mass to help the burn through calories. Early obesity invariably becomes permanent obesity for most people.

This is probably why the resident populations of nations with relative prosperity can easily pick up habits early in life that precipitate the obesity crisis. The stereotypical immigrant is one who is fleeing a zone of relative stress and discord—environments that are not conducive to enjoying the fruits of one's labor. Most immigrants are also more likely to come from backgrounds that were not luxurious. Gluttonous living escaped them, especially during the developing years, and they were thus protected by their meagre means from the morbidity of becoming obese. Their children now growing up under more prosperous circumstances, however, are lacking in this protection.

Age-Related Changes

The teenage years are marked with rapid changes in the developing individual's physical and mental states and lifestyle choices. Almost all of it can be tied to the chemical alterations happening in their bodies. Hormone-secreting glands begin a series of hormone releases at levels almost unprecedented in that body. We are familiar with the effects of steroids on the development of athletes' bodies, especially through the many scandals that have come to light. In addition to the physical changes that occur, we are also familiar with the mood changes associated with the steroid intake: steroid rage or sudden and unpredictable, sometimes violent, outbursts of anger. These effects are pretty much similar to the mood fluctuations seen in developing teens. Body changes accompanied by unpredictable mood changes are akin to being on steroids. Why does this effect appear to taper off then by the time individuals mature into early adulthood?

The explanation for that is complex. To some extent it has to do with the tapering down of some of those hormones that then continue to diminish gradually throughout their lives. By the time they get to their middle-age years and senior-adult years, the drop in hormone secretion becomes significant enough that some individuals might need to be supplemented by hormone replacement therapy. But a large part of the explanation is that over the years of teenage development, teenagers' bodies are constantly exposed to elevated levels of hormones through-out the teenage period, and their bodies undergo permanent modification in their ability to deal with those elevated levels. Thus, by the end of the teenage period, the reaction to the flood of chemicals of body's own making becomes less provocative. This is much like what happens to alcoholics in the early stages when they discover that they need ever-increasing doses of alcohol to attain or maintain an effect. Their bodies also adapt to accommodate the incorporation of the new chemical at regular frequency. Similarly, we develop a tolerance to increased production of chemicals from within. Eventually that becomes the new status quo within our bodies. As we approach middle age and old age, the organs responsible for hormone and steroid production begin to wane, and this change, once again, upsets the state of equilibrium we had previously gotten used to. Once again we are in for mood fluctuations, our bodies behaving incomprehensibly, and all in all another round of misery.

Every time a chemical is added to our bodies it interacts with our bodies, produces effects, and then gets destroyed and discarded, and our bodies reset back to their original chemical composition. What happens if we keep administering the chemical repeatedly and frequently? The body then has to contend with the chemical's presence more or less as a permanent ingredient. Eventually it has to modify itself to accommodate this ingredient. The imagery I like to conjure up to explain this point is as follows.

Imagine a glass of colored red gel, not a hard gel but a runny gel. Now to this you add a gel solution of blue color. Being gels they two will not mix outright immediately. In the beginning you will see the two distinct colors—red gel with a slowly swirling mass of blue gel, which will begin to thin out at the edges as it branches out in ever-thinning tentacular and filamentous wavy extensions into the red. Eventually they will all get mixed up and produce a purple gel. In my mind, that is what the human body is functionally doing. Instead of a glass jar I imagine the same action taking place within a porous membranous sack. Now an occasional entrant is usually cleaned out of the porous jar through a method of filtration, and the red gel is restored to its original composition. If the blue gel is constantly being introduced, then at some point in time structural changes within the gel jar will attempt to accommodate the blue gel, and eventually the innate composition will change to a purple gel.

This is, in fact, true for any ingredient we put into our bodies. Even food group chemicals can change the body irreversibly. Sugar is easily digested and used. But too much sugar along with other calories can precipitate a burnout of the insulin-producing organ, resulting in diabetes. Fats lead to obesity and deposition of fatty plaque in various tissues of the body, including the heart, resulting in heart disease. Too much protein becomes a load on the liver and kidneys, not to mention its ability to contribute to cholesterol increases. Once these permanent changes are in place, then even the reversal of habits will not reverse the buildup of side effects. Alcohol, drugs—prescribed or recreational—occupational chemical exposure, and chemical absorption through skin contact are all examples of the kinds of chemical introductions into the body that we have to contend with in our daily lives.

The chemicals from within our own bodies, like hormones, steroids, and opiate-like endorphins, are also treated by the body the same way. Most of these have a daily-regulated secretion schedule to adhere to, while some are released into the body on a need-to-have basis. The dramatic changes we see are either during the teenage growth phase when the secretions are suddenly and unpredictably ramped up and then toward the middle and old-age years when they are curtailed. The bag of chemicals changes its composition dramatically during the teenage years. Using the colored gel analogy, it is the gel would be almost rainbow colored due to the introduction of new chemicals.

Lifestyle is dictated, to a large extent, by the state of prosperity, habits, and novelty effect. In any society not in a state of great compositional change, there is a certain element of inertia in how people go about their daily lives. In the rich nations and the poor nations, where there is a certain stability of circumstances and lifestyle habits, food choices are relatively stable and unchanging with time. The status of health in these nations is more dependent on the levels of poverty, basic infrastructure, and health care status. There is a certain innate percentage of people with obesity issues and addiction issues.

People who have been exposed to reasonable good living through many generations are likely to have developed lifestyle and food habits that are relatively healthy, which they then tend to maintain and perpetuate. People who have been living within extremely limited means or who come from a background of limited consumption resources, might, on being exposed to a more luxurious lifestyle, end up overindulging in consumption. Besides, they are also more likely to be seduced by every new novelty they are exposed to. Most individuals in developing nations have grown up with the mindset for premium valuation for food, particularly meat products and sweets, as these are bound to be expensive and rationed to them due to their limited means. Upon attaining some measure of economic prosperity, however, the easiest and usually the first changes they make to their lifestyle habits are in the food habits they indulge in. This explains the sudden rise in obesity in nations like India and China recently.

Countries like the United States have a peculiar situation. The origins of this nation's population and its continued growth make it one of the few nations on this planet with this problem—the problem being that of being an immigrant nation. The other predominant immigrant nations are Canada and Australia. The United States was populated predominantly by people leaving other nations under duress or as a result of people's flight from unfavorable circumstances. Most who entered the nation came from backgrounds of economic hardship. Most old families grew up with the new nation through hard times, and because of that they developed a lifestyle of frugal existence. Obesity was never an issue till after the Second World War. Post Second World War saw the largest and the longest economic boom time for the nation. With this newfound prosperity and with it dramatically lowering food costs, the nation began an existence of self-indulgent living.

The economic success resulted in a problem with two heads. First was the creation of a work ethic that worshipped the concept of work as being the purpose of living, and second was the arrival of the fast-food culture and subsidized food production, leading to cheaper foods. The new work ethic gradually destroyed the concept of free time and made vacation and family time an unwelcome trait. People were encouraged to spend as much of their time being productive and hence at work. The desire to get rich was touted as laudable. Everyone, man or woman, signed onto this new paradigm. The result was less time for self and families away from work. Cooking food at home, as a result, has become either a chore or luxury for many families. Enter into this equation the concept of fast food, a high-calorie, low-cost alternative to cooking at home. This change in both lifestyle and food habits created within this wealthy nation the paradox of becoming wealthy but without the benefits of enjoying the wealth at home. To this mix add the arrival of new immigrants every year. Most of them come from relatively poor places. The exposure to lifestyle here in itself is a novelty-filled experience. Indulgences that they had kept in check at home are celebrated here. While the food habits of the adults may not drift far from their own nostalgic comfort zones, immigrants' children will be showered with the food and other items of instant gratification that they had no access to growing up in their native lands. This results in the descendant generation becoming prone to becoming self-absorbed with a touch of narcissism. Obesity-fueling food and lifestyle habits are permitted as rewards of finally making it into the population ranks of the richest nation in the world.

Addicts

Why do we participate in the intake of chemicals that alter our sense of reality? What makes such an alteration enjoyable enough that we wish to repeat the activity? Why do some of us easily succumb to the allure of a chemically induced altered state of consciousness while others are able to escape its hold? Finally, why does using alcohol and drugs for long periods change our bodies and minds permanently?

The answers to the first two questions are largely in the fields of philosophy and behavioral sciences. As to the latter two questions, it probably has a bit to do with our genetics and bit with the chemistry that plays out in our bodies. Much like the examples given earlier with regard to obesity and age-determined hormonal changes, the intake of recreational chemicals and alcohol also plays with the chemical balance of the body. The infrequent dabbler in these habits will not retain any permanent change to his or her body chemistry. But the addict will by his or her nature force the body's chemistry to change when chronically inputting these chemicals. These chemicals are all predominantly mood chemicals, meaning that the effect produced is measured by how they affect brain function.

The chemical environment of the body conditions the milieu in which the physical structures of the body develops. If the chemistry becomes skewed long enough, then it will cause the physical structures to change. Already there are gradual, irreversible changes happening to the physical components of the body as a result of the natural process of aging, which again is the result of changes in chemical production. Altered chemical environments add to this change and can result in irreversible changes to the physical components of the body, like the organs. Type 2 diabetes that is triggered usually as a result of a lifestyle of indulgences cannot be reversed to normalcy by having the individual resume healthy living. The chemical changes in the body have already imposed their effects on the insulin-producing organ long enough to cause it to burn out. This level of structural change as a result of exposure to prolonged chemical alterations cannot be repaired or reversed.

The brain is a critical organ in modulating the chemical environment in the body. It does this by a complex feedback loop with signals from the body, causing the brain to regulate the hormone-secreting glands and in other instances initiating direct nerve stimulations. Patients experiencing shortage of oxygen due to a condition called sleep apnea cause the brain to trigger through a combination of chemical and neuronal stimulation, increasing blood pressure, elevating the heart rate, and inducing a cough reflex to wake the person up from deep sleep. Another example of the brain regulating functions through altering the chemical environment is seen in people under chronic stress who develop blood pressure problems and diabetes. Stress triggers the release of hormones, which causes the blood vessels to constrict and stay constricted, causing blood pressure to elevate. Stress also triggers sugar fluctuations, and the resultant overload on insulin-secreting glands, not to mention the food indulgences that usually accompany stress, can precipitate diabetes.

The analogy of the bag of chemical soup is appropriate to brain function. Within the brain, as mentioned earlier, the vast majority of action happens due to electrochemical activity. All the multitude of chemical interactions results in the nerves talking to each other through small electrical pulses. The brain has a redundant supply of nerves, not all of which are functioning. If the chemical environment is altered, it causes some nerves to be suppressed and some to be selectively active. Mood alteration is due to this property. When they say that drugs are mind-bending in effect, that is exactly what is happening inside the brain—the selective firings of some parts over the others by altering the chemical soup composition by the drug. If the brain is subject to repeated alteration by these chemicals, then permanent structural changes will follow. The changes to blood flow affected by the chemical agent might cause irreparable damage to some parts of the brain, leading to death of nerve tissue. Unlike other tissues, nerve tissues cannot be repaired by replacement. The brain behaves much like having sustained localized mini strokes.

The issue of why some people become addicted relatively quickly while others do not might again have to do with a genetically predisposed chemical environment. Some individuals get drunk with as little as one glass of alcohol, while others can withstand two or three before the alcohol shows its effects. Another analogy to use here is one of a maze. There is a route through the maze that is to be followed for most normal nerve signals. In the presence of a drug, this maze becomes a little skewed; pathways that were previously open might now be impeded. The brain on drugs over time will cause the arrangement of the maze to change, causing alternate pathways for nerve conduction to develop. The degree to which this change is facilitated by the brain and the ease with which it does so might be the reason for the variations among people in the way that they react to alcohol and drugs. Some may have very robust maze structures that are resistant to change, and these individuals may not be affected by the drugs as profoundly. If mind-altering drugs do not bring about the mind alteration as expected, then the person is less likely to fall under the drug's spell. For some the phenomenon of the mind-altering experience might be unpleasant enough to not want to seek it. Thus, the resilience of the chemical mind labyrinth dictates the addiction potential among people.

Thus, getting back to the primary question about obesity in the United States, did the body chemistry of the people who originated genetically outside of the United States change when they crossed over the oceans? In a manner of speaking, yes! Even though their native gene pool would have designed a body of a particular size, shape, and health propensities, the lifestyle choices made by them or for them by their parents possibly changed indeterminably the working chemistry of their bodies. Their "chemical soup gels" underwent a metamorphosis, and the result is the epidemic of obesity. With time I am certain their genetic structures will also undergo a permanent change for the worse.

But there is hope. If lifestyle choices through modification of one's chemistry can change one's body type permanently in a single lifetime, then the reverse can also be true for those individuals' children. It will unfortunately involve a gathering of information from the concerned folks in the education and health care systems and working in close coordination with motivated citizenry and politicians and the food industry to change the way we eat, drink, and enjoy life through activities. I say unfortunately because that very activity will be fought tooth and nail by those choosing to profit from maintaining the status quo by calling such endeavors "socialistic," "intrusive," "privacy threatening," "big-brotherly in scope," etc.

twelve

Who is your Tribe?

As an immigrant to a country halfway across the planet from my birth country, I get to meet other immigrants, a lot of whom are like me, first-generation immigrants. I have been fascinated by the relative ease with which some have shed their affiliation to their country of origin and claimed an entirely new sense of place. The question "Where are you from?" is answered in a variety of ways. Some indicate the exact country and maybe even the region of the country where they are from, while others allude to the part of the adopted country they reside in. Some hold deep nostalgic and family ties with their land of origin, and some believe that they were born there by mistake and that they actually belong right here in their newfound home.

This sense of home and family and belonging is so variable. In a country like the United States, some elements of incompatibility, such as abject poverty, lack of access to information, discriminatory attitudes, and employment prospects, to a large extent have already been dealt with through social programs, technological achievements, and implementation of laws. These are most likely the drivers of the decision that began the journey of emigration for most people. But for others the driving force may have been the comfort of distance from an unfavorable home environment. But all of these individuals have had to make a deliberate attempt to unshackle their emotional, financial, and familial ties to their place of birth. This is a task not easily accomplished, and yet thousands seem to have done it. I am curious as to how these individuals have compensated for the loss of the sense of belonging that they may have had in their places of origin. How do they excommunicate themselves from their "tribe" of birth, and how do they replace that loss with a new sense of place and family in their new land?

There are over six billion humans living on Earth at the time of writing this essay. Most of them at their time of birth are assigned the "tribe" they belong to. We go about our daily lives paying scant attention to the implications of this de-facto membership to a relatively exclusive club (i.e., one's tribe). We never really question our connections until we are put in a position to sever them. All these existential ponderings of who we are and who our family is and where do we belong routinely and predominantly plague the mobile segments of our population, such as the emigrants and the immigrants.

For an emigrant, the roots of origin are deep and fed with a healthy dose of nostalgia. Despite wanting to leave their hometowns for better prospects elsewhere, their sense of home will still be associated with the home they left behind. This affinity will in time become less tenuous. The longer emigrants stay away from their origin source, the more likely they will be to adopt new habits and desires and a circle of friends and acquaintances that will eventually make them feel more at home in their new location. At this point, the identity of where they belong has entered a critical stage of flux. Now they are not certain of who and where their tribe is—the place of old familiarity or the current place of certainty.

This is a quandary from the ancient times and is still valid in today's world. In deciding one's tribe, one has to reconcile the nostalgia of the old with the satisfactions of the current life. Issues of family, loyalty to a nation or sovereign, and what is expected of them in return for being accepted into this new tribe are all questions that weigh on emigrants minds and consciences.

Of all the species on this planet, we are the only ones who are limited in our abilities to move around and choose a place to settle down in because of the restrictions imposed on unfettered movement and settling by our own laws. When each of us was born, there was no option to choose for ourselves which tribe we wanted to belong to. It is only when we get to a certain age that we begin to ask these fundamental questions and make decisions on choosing to stay or translocate. But even within that context, we have to deal with the logic of national boundaries, nationality, travel permits, residence permits, etc. As a member of a natural species to this planet, does that not seem strange that we should impose these ridiculous restrictions, especially since none of these nations had any say in our coming into existence in the first place?

Historically, due to our penchant for resorting to violence to solve our differences and waging war at the drop of a hat, it made sense to demarcate the physical confines of each independent nation and then manage those peripheries with armies. It made moving about a little constrained, but that was the price to pay for a modicum of peace. In peace, commerce could thrive and the native economies could function. The boundary demarcations, identifying members of the nation and protecting the sovereignty, were all done to preserve the larger context of a functioning state with its internal economic dynamics, and by doing so the nations could maintain peaceful coexistence, which would be an essential ingredient in long-term planning and which hopefully would lead to prosperity. That in essence is what any king, regent, or ruler was charged with by the nation's citizens.

The origin of modern humans and their spread across the world is believed to have begun in the Horn of Africa. In the sixty thousand years since the first successful migration began, we have populated most corners of the globe's landmasses. In the interim period, we have evolved to develop characteristic local traits of features, languages, cultures, and mythologies. Every corner of the world where the humans arrived began their existences through small communities. This tightly knit community of individuals, through multiple generations of existences, has developed a bond and a symbiotic relationship to the land they have gotten familiar with. These native populations are the primary nidus from which our modern nations have risen.

From the earliest days, the humans who banded together remained loyal to one another within the group. They identified with each other with a sense of familiarity enhanced through multiple shared experiences endured through the migratory journey, culminating in setting roots down on a piece of land. This community then grew by assimilating new migratory travelers as much as by breeding. The newcomers would have to abide by the rules laid out by the original settlers until they paid their dues in time, and then they would become a part of the original group. The amount of immigrant blood the community received would have varied depending on where the settlement was located (i.e., If the group was en route to other places and settlements, it would have received a significant amount of transitory migrants, few of whom might have decided to settle in.). The identity of the community would have changed with the speed at which it accommodated the new blood in, but through time, a certain flavor would have emerged that would have become distinctive for that community. Some of it might have been forced identity by the will of the elders, while some of it might have been regional specificity. For example, mountain dwellers would have a lifestyle unlike beach dwellers.

All in all, as communities developed, along with their identity, a sense of place and belonging also became established. This was usually an affirmation of the human bonds that developed. This human relationship web is what provided an individual with a sense of home and people. This was the first stage of establishing the identity known as tribe. The closer knit the community was and the lesser it got new blood by way of immigrants or through marriages, the more insular it became, and its identity would become that much more exclusive.

Geographical boundaries played a significant role in the formations of these early community identities. Multiple establishments of human villages would have interacted with one another though trade and marriage as long as they were within reach by easy methods of transportation. These groups of villages would eventually develop their common language or variation of language in time. They will share a common set of folklore, religion, and mythological tales. This is how the next layer of identity became established, one of language and kinship. The term *provincial*, meaning "to belong to a province" developed, as there were now provinces of villages and towns. Modern-day nations have been stitched together from hundreds to thousands of such ancient provincial communities.

Another layer of unification would have been on the grounds of sharing common theological beliefs. Religious belief was local in flavor for the longest time until the import of religions that sprang from the deserts of what we now consider as the Middle East.

The final layer would have been the group's response to a common enemy who threatened them with conflict as a means of compensating for depleting their resources within their geographical area. One set of criteria helped in solidifying early communities, including common food, language, religion, culture, and intermarriage, while other criteria, such as conflicts and geographical boundaries, established the confines of these unified communities by excluding their hostile neighbors. Thus rose the earliest kingdoms.

History then allowed the kingdoms to grow or recede with the fortunes of time. Today we see the result of this history in the nations that exist with clearly demarcated boundaries still recognized by most nations. These nations' sense of sovereignty and identity is mutually recognized and protected. Every one of these nations, other than the new immigrant nations of the Americas and Australia, are an amalgamation of many smaller provincial communities dating back in some cases to antiquity. The current identity of a tribe is now a national identity; it is a shared identity of language, food, culture, and to some extent, religion, under the larger arc of the common history of its ancestors.

According to the way history has played out, our homes, and by extension our tribes, are our reference points when discussing origins rather than the nation they became a part of. Therefore, if you visited a nation and asked someone where he or she was from, that individual would tell you of a province they came from. If the same query was asked of a person within a province, he or she might be more specific in alluding to a particular town or village. Within the town or village, the individual would claim his or her roots from a particular family. But when you ask someone at an international level, he or she usually points to the country of origin as being the land he or she belongs to. So the answer to which tribe one belongs to is usually dependent on a person's level of separation from his or her point of origin.

So are the citizens of any particular country truly representative of that country? I take the history of modern India as a good example in which to navigate through the effects of time in the development of one's identity. For instance, are all Indians who come from the subcontinent in South Asia similar? At first blush, to a non-Indian this might appear to be true. The commonalities of religion, spices in food, and dress codes will make it appear as if all Indians from South Asia are all cut from the same cloth. But the nation of India was stitched together from dozens of small kingdoms into a republic only as late as 1947. There are somewhere between twenty to thirty different official languages in the nation, each with its own unique script, grammar, etc. The number of dialects and regional languages might be in the hundreds. Though the majority religion is Hinduism, the practice is so varied that religious customs of certain regions are unique to them only. The state of Kerala has religious festivals and mythologies unheard of in other parts of the country. Food is another item of extensive variation, and with strong regional characteristics.

Based on the original description of the origins of tribe identity, it would appear that a country like India is actually composed of hundreds of distinct and unique tribes of people because of the apparent dissimilarities in language, food, cultural beliefs, and even dress patterns. The common elements of uniformity to the eyes of the outsider are not really that closely linked on closer examination. How then is it possible to impose a unifying national identity on this large a population of people who appear to have more elements of nonconformity among themselves?

Geographically, the region is cut off from the rest of the world by being sandwiched between the Himalayan Mountains in the north and west, the deep and thick forests of the Eastern Ghats mountains to the east, and the oceans to the south. This historically unique hard-to-access landmass is the result of a geological drift of the tectonic plate of the subcontinent of India northward until it slammed into the southern bit of Asia, causing the relatively new mountain ranges of the Himalayas to crop up. (This impact is still ongoing, and it is the reason for the gradual increase in height of the mountain ranges that is being recorded yearly). So within the context of the subcontinent of India, south of the Himalayas, the people developed themselves with minimal interaction with the rest of the world until the opening of the maritime routes to the southern ends and the establishment of trade routes through the mountain passes in the north. The earliest arrival of modern humans into this landmass is estimated to have been about sixty thousand years ago. But for the longest time immigration into this landmass was by fits and starts, what is called the "pastoral invasion." Mass migration was impossible because of the inhospitable terrain that buffered the borders. Pastoral migration, and later the invading armies of neighboring countries, accounted for the gradual introduction of outside cultures and traits to this land. But until the establishment of advanced technologies of mass transport and seafaring traditions, large-scale interactions were not possible. Trade routes to the west were established as early as the 30 BC. The east trade route, particularly with the courts of Chinese kingdoms, dates back to 350 BC.

Alexander is the first of many who attempted to gain entry with a large army population. That was in 326 BC. This was only partially successful as it ended in what is today's Pakistan. The next successful invasion was by the Mahmud of Ghazni in 1001 AD. But these were mostly raids to loot and pillage. The military did not come to conquer. The next big influential wave of invading foreign blood was in the fourteenth century under Tamerlane. Since that time India has received frequent visitation by foreign invaders and traders by land and sea. Thus, until 350 BC this land had been relatively underinfluenced by the rest of the world and allowed to quietly absorb the foreign influences that visited it through trade or through gradual eastward migration of new settlers. The speed of interaction and contact with foreigners speeded up after the fourteenth century with the Mughal and later the British conquests.

A multitude of individual tribe nations coexisted for the longest time, sometimes under the sovereign rule of one king or another. Kingdoms rose and fell. But the tribes continued their existences. Their earliest religious practices formed the seeds that in time would form the primordial religion that would later grow into the modern Hinduism. The first religious schism in this culturally vibrant set of people was with the introduction of Islam and later Christianity. Both of these religions managed to exist independent of the larger Hindu context. All previous beliefs that entered the land with the migrants were eventually co-opted by the native religions, a precursor to modern-day Hinduism. Today the population of this subcontinent of people is divided among seven nations: Afghanistan, Pakistan, India, Sri Lanka, Bangladesh, Nepal, and Bhutan. The national boundaries that have been established are more a result of political machinations than strict boundaries of tribe nations. India and Pakistan share communities across their border. The border splintered ancient communities, and with that a break in the identity of a regional tribe has ensued.

Today a citizen of India has much in common with other fellow Indians in that both are all members of a land whose people, by default, cannot be mistaken to belong to any other tribe groups of the world. They cannot be mistaken to belong to Europe, Africa, or the rest of Asia. They have a majority religion that is unlike the other majority religions of the world, especially those of Abrahamic origins. Their food is uniquely spiced with indigenous tropical spices of some fame. Thus, the modern Indian identity is one of exclusion from other identities. Since its independence, the nation has worked hard to create the ethos of a pan-Indian identity. But the "tribes" that constitute the nation still retain their individualism within the larger context of a national identity. Here again religious identity has also become secondary to regional identities. Thus, you have Indian citizens of all faiths still claiming their Indian identity through their more dominant regional affiliations. They are first members of a particular group within a state and are more recognized by a commonality of their regional language than by their religion. They are all, after all, the descendants of the same group of people, some of whose ancestors switched their religious preferences in the recent past. There are Christian and Muslim families that have distant relatives who are still practicing their ancestral religion, which is now recognized as Hinduism.

This dynamic is different in the nations that have come into existence through large immigrations. The Americas and Australia have been and are still the choice destinations for global populations running away from some incompatibility at home. Of these, the United States, Canada, and Australia get the lion's share of being the global destination choices for wannabe emigrants. Though these nations did and still do possess indigenous tribes, they have, through the decades, been outpopulated by the large droves of immigrants entering these lands. In the past two centuries, the nations of these countries have become majority immigrant nations. Here in the United States there are no historical tribe communities that new immigrant descendants can claim their domicile status to, hence here there have been many different modes of compensating for the absence of traditional tribe identity.

The first universal tier of identification among all immigrants and their descendants is one of a national citizenship. This honor is felicitated by identifying with the country's flags, colors, anthems, and other open forms of expression of patriotism. The provincial identity, if it exists, is usually the second tier. The other identity that they clothe themselves in is with regard to membership in associations, such as religious orders or particular churches, social organizations, political organizations, networking clubs, etc. A pointed difference between the way an Indian citizenship differs from that of an American or Canadian or Australian citizenship is that in India, no matter where one eventually settles down, he or she is usually first and foremost recognized by the language he or she owns up to as his or her native tongue. The individual's provincial loyalties take precedence over any national allegiances. Thus, an individual will be recognized for the regional language group he or she comes from, such as a Tamil, Punjabi, Bengali, etc. The Indian identity is secondary. In the immigrant nations, the citizenship identity, especially among the immigrants, appears to be the primary identity and sometimes the only identity. Here the mythology of belonging to the larger "tribe" is maintained by frequently dabbling in patriotic rituals to empower citizens to proudly take ownership of their national identity. Thus, in these nations, lively display of patriotic fervor is common.

Like the India experiment, a similar unification process has been attempted and is still in progress in Europe. Economic stress and strains have made it necessary for the individual nations of Europe to band together under a pan-European banner. They have even instituted a common currency, the euro, and have done away with a lot of the travel restrictions and requirements within the continent of Europe for the citizens of the nations that have banded together. Here again, like in the Indian context, the European identity is secondary to the individual ("tribe") national identities of being French, Italian, Spanish, etc.

In the modern world, affiliation with a group of individuals—the contemporary equivalent of the tribe—is about sharing mutual common interests, familiarity, and shared values and is less about being related by blood. This new tribe is one of opportunistic symbiosis due to a common locale of residence and less about multigenerational loyalties. For some, this tribe might be the circle of friends or members of a church group, a networking social organization like the Rotarians, members of a hobby activity, or family of children from one school.

The old demarcations, geographical or social, that would have preserved the authenticity of a tribe's composition are becoming increasing less relevant to the mobile individual in the modern times. The individual human potential, if it is to be allowed to blossom unhindered, needs to be set free of the yoke of tradition. While the old tribe structure provided a sense of continuity and predictability, it was also very rigid in tolerating the individual expressions of potential not in keeping with traditional expectations and mores.

Today, if allowed, anyone can travel anywhere in the world to explore their dreams and desires and hopefully find a place where they may explore their niche. For this to happen, there has to be a serious global rethink on the nature of country borders, work and travel permits, and immigration policies. It would benefit everyone if the world would accommodate free and purposeful travel for those seeking gainful employment anywhere in the world. Racist attitudes and paranoia of loss of national or regional identity by the absorption of too many foreigners keep the pressure up to preserve the national borders and maintain arduous immigration policies. Domestic health of individual economies might play a role in the decisions of travel and work limitations on the global population. But if an individual were to find a place where he or she could come into his or her own and exploit that hidden potential, it would benefit everyone, including the local economies. Unimpeded tourism travel would be a boon to the host nation, and besides, who are we to impose restrictions on the movement of people who want to see the bountiful diversity of this planet on which each and every one of us has equal rights?

Thus, whether we reside in a traditional society or we are a member of the mobile population destined for the shores of some new vibrant nation, we all, by default, belong to a "tribe," or we substitute as best as we can the feeling of belonging to a "tribe" through our circle of friends and acquaintances and our involvement in social organizations.

Now, who is your tribe?

thirteen

Altruism

Are humans capable of being truly altruistic? Is the behavior of altruism consistent with our self-protective instincts? What possible evolutionary advantage is there to being altruistic? Before answers to these questions can even be contemplated, one must be clear about what the word *altruism* refers to. The traditional definition is one of acting in absolute selflessness to help someone or something. In other words, altruism encompasses actions that benefit others with no tangible benefits to oneself with even probably a net loss to self being expected.

One of the arguments against the notion of true altruism is that most of what we do is usually due to some internal motivation. The fact that the action originates from an internal place within us indicates that, in performing the task or action, there is a yet unperceived benefit to us. For example, let's examine a heroic event: a building on fire with a trapped child or animal inside that motivates a group of individuals, untrained in the skills of firefighting, to rush into the building to save the child or animal. Such an action, no matter how foolhardy it might appear, is bound to be acknowledged with gratitude and cheers, provided nothing untoward happens to either the savior or the saved. So what motivates the person or persons to take such risks to save someone or something with whom they probably have had no prior association? Is it that in the act of saving they are somehow acknowledging the teachings of an upbringing, faith, or just their personal moral compass? At the moment of decision making that would have preceded the action of running into a burning building, the individuals would have to have weighed the benefits of their actions versus the risks, all in a time frame where any hesitation or diffidence would be counterproductive. With so much resting on practically split-second decision making, how much of that would be based on prior indoctrinations of values and how much would be due to the need to respond to an internal trigger, to act without too much introspection?

How about the more mundane actions of charity on an individual basis, like the personal time and effort one commits to things like running homeless shelters, soup kitchens, etc.? In these actions too there is no financial reward or awards or any other form of acknowledgment anticipated. Would these be considered as examples of altruism?

More pertinently, is there an evolutionary element in the altruistic behavior? We are conditioned to reflexively perform to protect our own interests. This element of selfishness is critical to individual members of our species when charting their own destiny, while being hyperaware of the inherent dangers of doing things alone. Therefore, we have created this social interaction mode wherein we all together contribute to the general well-being of the collective, and in doing so, the collective will ensure that an individual's interests are taken care of. In this mode, it is not the goodness of one's heart that forces one to behave in a manner suitable to the collective as a whole, but rather the expectation of mutually reciprocity. Therefore, risking one's own life to save that of another has a larger implication of the reverse being expected if the roles were reversed.

Our responses to conditions involving children and pets might have more to do with something primordial than a true altruism instinct that some would consider to be a more advanced thought process—or is it? Some experts have deemed that the affinity and protectiveness with which we deal with children might have to do with protecting one's own bloodline. Sounds like a lot of academic nonsense, right? We cannot accept the fact that decisions we make have any other motives than the obvious immediate one, and to consider those decisions to be the result of some primordial equivalent to a knee-jerk reaction sounds preposterous. Rational thought will not explain the ridiculous levels to which we expend our time and efforts to routinely protect our own or our impulsive reaction in confronting danger when it involves our own children, even if it means putting ourselves in harm's way for them. Furthermore, how does one explain the similar reaction by strangers to unrelated children and pets in danger? I suppose it is by extension of the association projected that one empathizes with those in danger. Vulnerable kids stimulate the same response zones in the brain irrespective of their parentage. Is it a collective preservation strategy? Pets appear to play the role of pseudo-children. They are nonvocal and vulnerable because of the circumstances they usually find themselves in on account of their association with adults/masters.

A simple demonstration of how our minds work in regard to kids is as follows. Imagine a scenario that you walk into unprepared. In a public arena like an airport, you encounter the following scene: a child on the floor covering his head and sobbing quite forcefully. Standing beside the child is an extremely angry and loud parent yelling at the child. The child appears to be in complete submission and is offering no resistance. In addition to the aggression from the parent is the issue of the demonstration of such rage at a defenseless child in a public domain. Imagine the fear, sorrow, and hurt from such public humiliation that the child might be suffering. Does it make you uncomfortable, perhaps a bit annoyed with the parent, a bit sorry for the child? Most people will feel a sense of empathy toward the child and may even fault the parent for his or her bullying demeanor. What if you had happened on the same scene from the very beginning and got to witness the buildup to the parental meltdown? What if the child was throwing a fit and was being loud and obnoxious and he was deliberately ignoring all attempts to mollify him, and then finally the behavior resulted in the parent snapping and punishing the child? Now, does the observer feel the same pangs of pity and sorrow for the child? Or does the child look more like a brat and not so much a victim? Context illuminates viewpoints. The point of this example is to show how, at an instinctive level, we feel the need to be protective of a child, especially when the child shows signs of being defenseless and vulnerable. The same appears to be the case with animals in distress.

These "pseudo-kids" appear to trigger the same empathy pathway in the brain. Is this a primordial behavioral pattern?

Here is another consideration to take into account when looking for altruism reasons. Not all people are naturally prone to altruistic tendencies. By the same token, not all people find children or pets to be cute, vulnerable, or in need of protecting. They would much rather have that responsibility fall on others' shoulders. Is it because they have evolved out of the protective mindset, or are they lacking in the ability to empathize, or are they just too self-absorbed to care about others' inconveniences? It appears that in order to be altruistic one has to have the ability to empathize and want to help. Why is this so? Does it instill in them a sense of superiority stemming from the higher purpose they allude to in undertaking any charitable action? Or does it make them feel good to have done some good?

I believe that any action we take has to have a personal connection attached to it to make it successful. Taking ownership of a task is in essence that personal commitment to the task. There is a psychological positive return to be expected for a job well attempted. For the sanguine, the end result by itself is not the reason for participation in an activity. It is the activity in itself that provides context and satisfaction. There are those who are results-oriented, and there are those who are process-oriented. I think the process-oriented people need the interaction derived from the process to feel accomplished. It appears that those process-oriented individuals involved in acts of altruism seem to be more particular about the process of helping than they are concerned with whether the actions they took truly had a lasting effect on the person needing help. The people who are not willing to contribute their personal time and energy to helping others are operating from their moral code, which is different from those who volunteer easily. They might have a reticent personality and believe in helping only if they are directly approached and requested, or they might be ones who do well in solitary endeavors and who might be uncomfortable in affiliating with large groups of people. They might be terrified of children and not certain of how to handle a child. Most individuals who shirk the need to be generous with their time and effort have personal obstacles to surmount before they can make themselves available to altruistic enterprises. For them the personal negatives that they need to contend with are far greater than any possible positives they might encounter. If such people do perform altruistic missions, then I would contend that they are the ones who are truly being altruistic as they are not enjoying anything positive but are having to battle their personal demons in order to participate.

Aside from kids and pets, the desire to reach out and help someone, therefore, appears to depend on the ability of one to empathize and the desire to be involved in a process of aiding and not being inhibited by personal constraints. The element of empathy is the most critical one. It is the one that most aid organizations hope to capitalize on when they seek donations or help in an effort (i.e., natural disaster relief or food drives or aid to victims of war and conflict zones). Here again one can appreciate the ease of recruiting help for some endeavors over others. People who have lived through a natural disaster would be more likely to pitch in and help victims of another natural disaster. People who have suffered at the hands of gunmen in a mass shooting incident will more likely band together to provide support for one another and other victims of gun violence. But people in war-torn areas have difficulty getting the kind of aid that people who are recovering from natural disasters get relatively easily. Part of this has to do with the distance, physically and emotionally, that these conflict zones have from the rest of the peaceful world. But this changes dramatically if the rest of the peaceful world gets exposed to images of horror and suffering from the conflict zones. When people see suffering, then they get to empathize more effectively than if they were to hear the same story without the benefit of accompanying images. The earthquake that did damage to the island of Haiti in 2010 elicited a very strong response from many world countries largely due to the visual documentation of the damage. The pictures from that region did more than all the write-up from the same region.

The obvious question is this: Why do we need to have personal exposure with hardship in order to recognize the need to help others enduring a hardship? In other words, why does empathy emanate best from a personal experience of suffering? People who have lived through poverty and struggled with effects of economic hardship are more sensitive to the needs of the poor. When someone expends personal time and energy to come to another's aid, what is the subconscious trigger that can be responsible for the decision to help? It is obviously not the result of any great rational thought where one weighs the pros and cons of action, does a risk assessment, and then decides what is considered an appropriate amount of commitment. That is too much thinking to do some impromptu good. Therefore, most likely, the stimulus for altruistic behavior is one of deep-seated impulse, most likely the contribution of the subconscious.

Empathizing with someone must begin with recognizing the plight of the person needing help. Recognition is usually the result of prior knowledge, either through becoming educated about a condition or having been exposed to the same condition previously. It is the rare person who can with their imagination alone understand the unfavorable circumstances to be able to feel what the person needing help might be enduring. The ones who have previously experienced a discomforting situation will have a visceral memory of the condition. (Soldiers returning from conflict experience an extreme form of memory called post-traumatic stress disorder. Here it is not the issue of empathy as much reliving the horrors of a traumatic experience.) In empathizing with someone, we might be in some measure reliving our own encounter with a similar traumatic incident. Thus, when we reach out to help someone, it might be a subconscious equivalent to reaching out to help ourselves. Thus, in indulging in acts of altruism, it is possible that we might be saying, *"I wish I had had someone to help me when I needed it. Now I am in a position to fulfill that need for someone else, and by doing so I am attempting to reach back to extend a helping hand to myself."* The act of altruism is more about the need for involvement by the altruistic than about the good the act might do for the person it is meant to help. Altruism, therefore, might be the ultimate manifestation of self-awareness and subconscious self-absorption rather than selflessness.

This might explain some of the extreme actions of altruism that we celebrate. Selfless or self-centered, the acts of altruism are still very welcome. We, as a species, claim our moral superiority and our humanity through examples of altruism.

www.ingramcontent.com/pod-product-compliance
Lightning Source LLC
Chambersburg PA
CBHW061738020426
42331CB00006B/1280